THE ZERO-CARBON HOUSE

THE ZERO-CARBON HOUSE

MARTIN GODFREY COOK

THE CROWOOD PRESS

First published in 2011 by
The Crowood Press Ltd
Ramsbury, Marlborough
Wiltshire SN8 2HR

www.crowood.com

British Library Cataloguing-in-Publication Data
A catalogue record for this book is available from the British Library.

ISBN 978 1 84797 262 0

Disclaimer
The author and the publisher do not accept responsibility, or liability, in any manner
whatsoever for any error or omission, nor any loss, damage, injury or adverse outcome of
any kind incurred as a result of the use of the information contained in this book, or
reliance upon it. Readers are advised to seek professional energy efficiency, architectural,
building and other advice relating to their particular property, project and circumstances
before embarking on any building or related work.

Frontispiece image: Lighthouse – viewed from the south-west.

Typeset by Jean Cussons Typesetting, Diss, Norfolk
Printed and bound in China by 1010 Printing International Ltd

Contents

DEDICATION

For Molly and Lucy

ACKNOWLEDGEMENTS

I should like to thank all the members of the RIBA Sustainable Futures Committee for their stimulating company over the years, not to mention the fierce email debates over the definition of 'zero carbon' and many other cutting-edge topics. Particular thanks are especially due to Bill Dunster OBE and Mark Elton RIBA for their help with material for the BedZED and Hyde House case studies, respectively. I think we have now reached a consensus on the definition of good architecture as the three ancient canons of Marco Polio Vitruvius plus sustainability. We will resist all attempts to place adjectives such as 'green', 'eco' and 'sustainable' in front of the term 'architecture' for as long as we meet!

I should also like to thank the many owners, architects and other agents of case study zero-carbon houses, who were generous with access and material, particularly John Christophers RIBA. John's refurbished and extended Victorian terraced house in Birmingham, England, gives a glimpse of the carbon-neutral future for the existing housing stock, in the United Kingdom and elsewhere for that matter – possibly even Birmingham, Alabama, USA.

Internationally, I am grateful to Michael Reynolds AIA for access to Earthships in the UK and abroad, and Jaime Lerner, architect and former mayor of Curitiba for his open discussion at the British Film Institute in London, after the screening of the documentary film *A Convenient Truth: Urban Solutions from Curitiba, Brazil* towards the end of 2009. The scientists and authors, Stewart Brand and Jim Lovelock, deserve particular mention for the insights that their consistently wise and thought-provoking books have provided me with over the years. The many other publications that have influenced me are given due credit at the end of this book.

Closer to home, I should like to offer my sincere thanks to Crowood for their sound advice and infinite patience during the preparation of this manuscript. Finally, infinite thanks are due to my family for their constant support, and I hope that this publication goes some small way to help to secure a sustainable future for the younger members of my wider family.

Preface

The idea of reducing your carbon emissions to zero is a challenging prospect, but far from impossible to do in your house, prospective or existing, old or new. Our domestic energy use and associated carbon dioxide emissions are a good place to start, as at least three-quarters of the houses we live in now will still be with us in 2050 – the year that dramatic carbon-reduction targets are usually set for. So, the impact of new dwellings is limited – maybe they should be less-than-zero carbon.

The imperative to reduce our collective environmental impact was never more important, as global population continues to grow and more people indulge in profligate lifestyles – business as usual is not an option, on an international level. Indulgent lifestyles are so last-century and threaten to deplete diminishing resources – it is churlish to reduce your carbon footprint at home and then splurge your reductions on luxuries such as long-haul air travel – take the train or ship instead!

Our behaviour is clearly an important aspect of our response to environmental warning signs, such as the depletion and extinction of animal species, many of which it is difficult to see how we could survive without, such as the humble bumble bee. This book gives some consideration to these aspects in its first and final chapters. But the main thrust is the zero-carbon house and how it is achievable in old or new building stock.

Chapter 2 gives a brief description of the evolutionary and theoretical attempts at zero-carbon houses, or zero-energy or autonomous houses as they were called in yesteryear. This quest started almost a century ago, just as we were becoming increasing less sustainable, due to cheap electricity and fossil fuels, and was spurred on by the energy crisis of the 1970s. There is much to learn from the history of the quest, and it is sobering to think that global population has doubled to seven million in the four decades since our last earnest attempts at domestic sustainability.

Chapters 3, 4 and 5 deal with existing, new and communities of zero-carbon houses – the latter is clearly an essential aim to release economies of scale in our quest to reduce our impact on the planet: one-planet houses for one-planet living, and survival. Chapter 5 is devoted to Earthships, first pioneered by the New Mexican architect, Michael Reynolds in the 1970s – for which he was in turn vilified and, latterly, praised by the American Institute of Architects. The recently produced documentary film of his quest, *Garbage Warrior*, is essential viewing.

Treat the earth well: it was not given to you by your parents, it was loaned to you by your children. We do not inherit the earth from our ancestors, we borrow it from our children.

Oglala Sioux proverb

CHAPTER 1

Zero Carbon

To be modern is to find ourselves in an environment that promises us adventure, power, joy, growth, transformation of ourselves and the world – and, at the same time, that threatens to destroy everything we have, everything we know, everything we are.

Marshall Berman (1982)

INTRODUCTION

'Climate change is the biggest threat that our civilization has ever had to face up to'. These words were uttered recently by Professor Sir David King in a BBC radio interview. The former Chief Scientific Advisor to the UK Government went on to say that he thought climate change was a bigger threat than terrorism – an existential threat, but one that we are not focusing upon – it is too abstract and seems far off into the future. We focus on threats like terrorism and nuclear weapons, as existential threats that are immediate and tangible. They are easier to focus on than the beguilingly abstract threats of global warming and climate change, which are also serious and increasingly immediate existential threats.

King went on to cite recent events that showed the existential threat of climate change, such as the summer of 2003, which was the hottest on record, and in which 32,000 people lost their lives. It was the largest single natural disaster in Central Europe in recent times, but it was not recorded as such because it played out over several weeks, rather than happening in a media-friendly instant. Although there is no doubt that the media plays its part in sensationalizing scientific predictions, not always helpfully, perhaps.

Sir David King was equally controversial in his views on the invasion of Iraq, and regarded oil as the primary driver for what he called the first of the modern 'resource wars' – a friendly government is needed in Iraq to ensure continued supplies of cheap oil, in his view. In particular, he cited the United States of America, who use roughly a quarter of the world's oil production and have an economy that is based on the availability of cheap oil. Iraq is geographically situated on a very large amount of the remaining conventional supplies of oil, a fact that was thrown into sharp relief by the need to drill a mile beneath the sea in the Gulf of Mexico, for closer reserves of oil – a technically challenging endeavour that can easily go badly wrong.

The USA is an easy target in terms of carbon addiction, but we are all mainlining on fossil fuels. The States could have ameliorated their image by signing Kyoto, but even those nations who did, such as Britain, are not meeting their targets. The UK Government recently admitted that they will fail to meet their 2010 carbon dioxide emissions targets. On a more positive note, Sir David does not view the recent conference in Copenhagen as a disaster for action on climate change – quite the contrary, actually. Although a global protocol was not produced, everyone turned up, including 150 heads of states and all the larger nations, and a document that takes us forward was formulated. Developing countries, such as Indonesia, have committed to reduce their carbon emissions by 26 per cent; Brazil said that they will stop all deforestation and start reforestation by 2025 – and a large part of our rising carbon dioxide emissions are from deforestation.

King was of the opinion that long-term infrastructure and the built environment were the most important issues, such as coal-fired power stations that should be replaced with power sources that do not emit carbon dioxide, for the next half-century. Renewable energy sources, such as solar, wind and water power are ways of doing this, but so is nuclear. That the latter may be a necessary evil, in the medium term, to reduce carbon

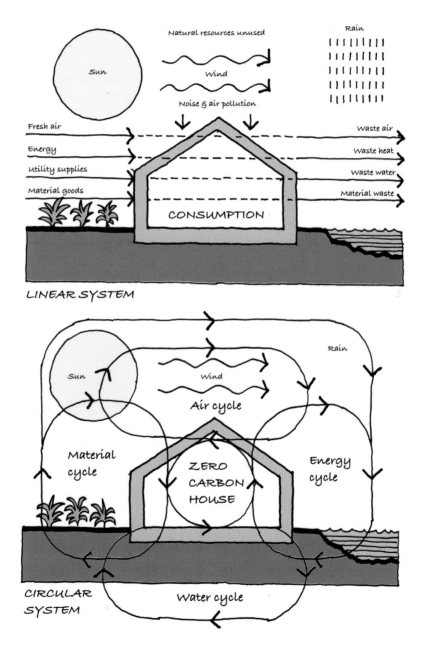

Linear versus circular systems – the holistic zero-carbon house.

emissions is a view held by an increasing number of eminent scientists, such as Sir David King, himself; James Lovelock, inventor of the Gaia theory; and David Mackay, who is the UK Government's chief advisor on climate change and global warming. Mackay is completely unconvinced that decarbonization with renewable energy alone can be done, and certainly not quickly enough. On less controversial ground, there is no doubt that we need to build a zero carbon-built environment – and there is no place like starting at home with a zero-carbon house.

PROGRESS AND GROWTH

At the beginning of the twenty-first century we find ourselves potentially careering towards ecological and environmental catastrophe on a global scale – which obviously also threatens concomitant social and economic disaster. The triple bottom line of the new mantra of sustainability is environmental, economic and social sustainability. In the case of the latter factor, the extraordinary progress of modernity, science and technology – spurred on by military rivalry at the worst of times and more benign technology races at the best of times – has

allowed a rapidly burgeoning global population growth. Our increasing numbers have, until recently, remained a taboo subject in sustainability circles – too sensitive a subject, perhaps, to admit that fecundity might have an impact on our targets to reduce our carbon emissions. This factor is now recognized and UN population growth projections are published that push out to the twenty-third century – mid-range estimates show an optimistic levelling of global population, eventually.

As it ever was, some would say, and it must have appeared a similar scenario a century or so ago when the previous century had wrought a quadrupling of the UK population, for example, with massively increased urbanization. The success of the industrial revolution's ability to feed its expanded population, through industrialized agricultural methods, made this possible – inconceivable to Thomas Malthus as he wrote his famous essay in 1798. Those historic times had their own problems of poverty, pollution and economics, but we are still linked to those old notions of progress through growth, fuelled by fossil fuels. Ironic then, that the first industrial mills were sited next to watercourses, as the only viable source of sufficient power before the invention of the steam

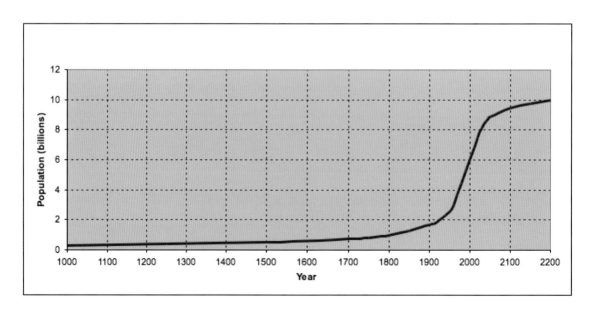

UN mid-range prediction of population growth until 2200.

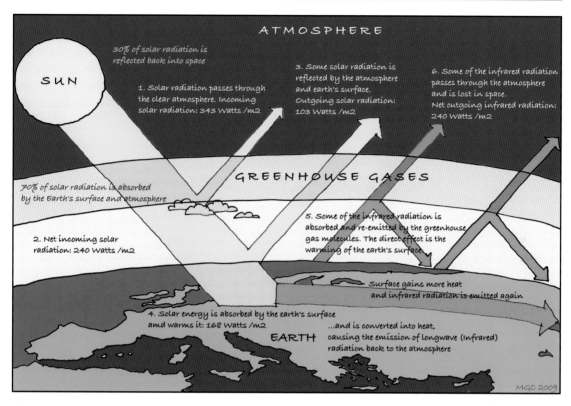

The greenhouse effect.

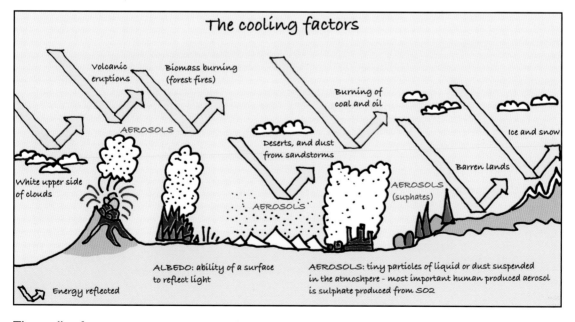

The cooling factors.

engine – a renewable energy world that we are now striving hard to reinvent.

We are also still linked to those historic times by our continuing population explosion, to the extent that global population is now doubling every forty years, has reached seven billion, and is set to rise to nearly ten billion by 2100 or earlier. The last two centuries of this extraordinary progress and growth was fuelled by fossil fuels, first mainly in the form of coal, and the last hundred years or so by oil and gas. The planet's finite fossil fuel resources took million of years to create, and

Fishy Business

We are currently fighting a war against the remaining stocks of fish in our oceans, and we are winning with the use of technology and efficient, but destructive, techniques such as beam-trawling that leave the ocean bed looking like a desert. Our once bountiful oceans are proving less sustainable than we thought, due to our continuous onslaught. In the early 1990s the apparently unlimited supplies of cod off the east coast of Canada were found to be on the point of extinction, and a moratorium on fishing was the only way to try and save them – they are not rebounding quickly. The situation is not much better in European waters, where relentless fishing of bluefin tuna has resulted in catches declining by 80 per cent over the past decade.

Large-scale industrial fishing began in about 1950, with the result that experts estimate that the once relative abundance of large fish is now reduced by about 90 per cent. These are clearly contentious claims and disputed by those with a vested interest – but there is consensus over many species, such as yellowfin and skipjack tuna in the Pacific Ocean. The latter are decimated, and the argument is only over the scale of the destruction – somewhere between 70 and 90 per cent reductions on 1950 baseline estimates. The basic problem is too many high-tech, industrial fishing boats, which are continuously and very effectively hunting down every known edible species of fish – too much demand pursuing an increasingly limited supply. Global fishing fleets could catch the world fish population four times over, and electronic and sonar equipment leaves fish with nowhere to hide.

Bluefin tuna has an ancient lineage and once sustained Roman legions in battle – it is now in the frontline itself, as the species is hunted to extinction. Additionally, spotter planes are being used to find shoals of bluefin, which are then fished out by fleets of boats. The fishing-out of certain species results in an unsustainable imbalance in local ecosystems, as their natural predators or prey species decline. This gives dubious benefits in some cases, such as the burgeoning population of lobsters in Finland, but also leads to phenomena such as jellyfish infestations in other waters. Oceans that were once full of large fish are now filling up with plankton.

Experts predict that, if current trends are allowed to continue, stocks of fish that we now eat could collapse by 2050. However, we understand much more about what is happening to fish populations than we did as little as five years ago, so we can do something about it. Alaska is a good example, where they are restricting their fishing fleets' capacity to the resource available, and giving fishermen limited seasons to fill their controlled quotas of fish. Consumers can control excesses by demanding to know where their fish comes from, how it was caught and whether it is endangered, to bring about positive changes. For example, pollock is a potential substitute, which should allow cod populations to increase – choices consumers make will have an effect on marine diversity.

Fish farming is an intensive agricultural solution, but it uses smaller, wild fish to feed larger species, such as salmon. Actually eating the smaller fish, such as anchovy and herring, is more sustainable and optimal. Marine reserves are also being established to provide sanctuaries and areas where commercial fishing is completely banned – but they will not completely solve the problem. Political will is necessary to bring about sustainable fishing policies, and the industry has to abide by them – and we must only eat sustainable seafood. Research suggests that fish droppings help oceans to absorb carbon dioxide – linking over-fishing with global warming and climate change.

12

ultimately come from the power of the sun, through photosynthesis in ancient vegetation. These unique reserves are effectively the ancient sunlight of past eons of time, which we are tapping into at a phenomenal and unsustainable rate as our numbers increase and 'carbonize'. Ironically, some of this carbonized industrialization also provides cooling factors to counter the familiar greenhouse effect diagram.

POPULATION

The word Malthusian conjures up an infamous and unpopular concept, originating as it does from the work of the Reverend Thomas Robert Malthus (1766–1834) and his essay on the principle of population first published in 1798, and then republished several times in successive revised editions until 1826. Malthus thought that the dangers of population growth would preclude endless progress towards a utopian society, summed up in his pronouncement that 'The power of population is indefinitely greater than the power of the earth to produce subsistence for man'. He thought that the increase of population is necessarily limited by the earth's means of subsistence; that population invariably increases when the means of subsistence increases; and that population would be kept equal to the means of subsistence, by what he called 'misery and vice'.

Malthus cited the geometric or exponential progression of population growth, which was already beginning in the early nineteenth century, as industrialization and urbanization burgeoned, contrasted with the arithmetic or straight-line growth of the means of subsistence or food supply. Malthus's detractors point to the fact that population has grown exponentially since he expanded his theories, and that he could not possibly have conceived of the technological advances that humankind has achieved, not least in the field of agriculture and food supply. However, the technological progress that has allowed human population to grow exponentially is heavily based on a carbon economy and finite fossil fuels. A reverse exponential curve could apply to our rapid depletion of these resources, particularly as population growth continues to explode.

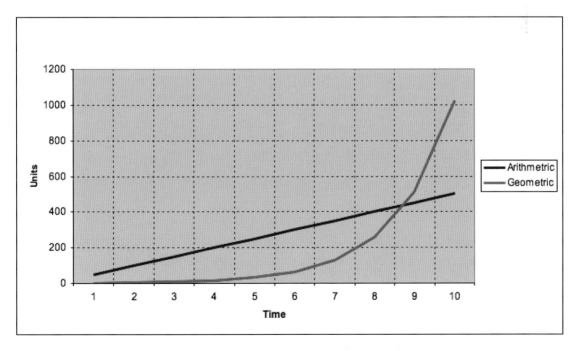

Exponential and linear progressions.

To Bee or Not to Bee

Bees arrived on the earth 20 million years before humanity, but now they appear endangered by our activities. Scientists have discovered that pollination levels have dropped by nearly a half in some plants over the last twenty years – this 'pollination deficit' could herald reductions in crop yields. The decline in the bee population is seen as the equivalent of the canary in the mineshaft – an indicator species to which we should pay some attention. They are essential to the reproductive process of most plants (about 80 per cent) as they cross-fertilize pollen from one flower to another. Climate change has probably created a seasonal mismatch between when flowers open and when bees emerge from hibernation.

The honeybee is our oldest friend, as one in every three bites of food depends on them – without them we are left with only rice, corn and wheat. Our livestock also depends on them for their diet. Their increasing and mysterious disappearance carries an important message for us – our activities are unsustainable. Bees in England are disappearing faster than elsewhere in Europe, with more than half of the hives dying out in the last two decades. The UK Government is funding a £10 million research programme to try and find out what the factors are behind the vanishing bees and other insects.

As our agricultural systems became industrialized, so did the industry of the bee hive, with industrial-scale hives being transported across countries and continents – from the almond groves of California to the blueberry fields of Maine, to seasonally pollinate such crops. A few years ago many beekeepers began noticing an alarming disappearance of their bees – many empty hives but with no dead bees in them. Scientists began to name the disastrous phenomenon 'Colony Collapse Disorder' (CCD), while attempting to get to the bottom of the malaise. The novelist Leo Tolstoy stated many decades ago that the workings of the honeybee hive were beyond our comprehension, but that didn't stop us experimenting with it to improve efficiency – splitting hives and artificially inseminating queen bees in our efforts to increase productivity.

The rate of attrition of the honeybee is high, with more than a third of the British bee population estimated to have disappeared. The number of beekeepers has declined to combine with disease, intensive and monocultural agriculture, and modern pesticides to decimate the humble bumble bee. Loss of the bees' natural environment, such as herb-rich meadows and heather moorland, over the last half-century has also reduced the number of bees. American scientists believe that all these stresses lead to a reduced immune system in bees – this, coupled with further distances to travel to find nutrition, leads to bees dying outside the hive, or possibly even losing their way and being unable to get back to their hives. Scientists at Sussex University are trying to decode the 'waggle dance' that bees make when returning to the hive, which is thought to inform worker bees of the location of food sources, giving the direction and distance to the source that the bee has just located.

The problem of environmental pollution was first mooted in the early 1960s by authors such as Rachel Carson, whose book *Silent Spring* referred to the death of songbirds as a result of pesticide poisoning, and the ensuing lack of birdsong. Pesticide chemicals were described by Carson as coming out of chemical warfare research during the Second World War. Almost accidentally, some of the chemicals were found to be fatal to insects

---

Most of the world's carbon-reduction targets are set as percentage reductions of historic levels, such as the year 1990, but as world population is doubling every forty years, it has increased by 50 per cent in the last twenty years – making population size a finally recognized and crucial factor in the battle against climate change and global warming. Many latter-day Malthusians, such as Professor

Al Bartlett, argue that the food supply that has ostensibly refuted Malthus's theories so far, is only made possible by the petrochemical industries and fertilizers, not to mention genetically modified crops. Bartlett points to what he calls the 'essential exponential', the geometric progression – if our use of finite resources such as oil and coal increases by even a small percentage, year-on-year,

and were then used as pest controls. She concluded that 'The control of nature is a phrase conceived in arrogance, born of the Neanderthal age of biology and philosophy, when it was supposed that nature exists for the convenience of man.... It is our alarming misfortune that so primitive a science has armed itself with the most modern and terrible weapons, and that in turning against the insects it has also turned against the earth'.

The use of pesticides on crops is thought have compromised bees' navigational abilities and weakened their immunity. French beekeepers have experienced similar hive collapses and claim to have identified specific pesticides that cause the problem. It takes several hundred worker bees to gather the pollen from around 2 million flowers to produce a 1lb (450g) pot of honey. Honey is one thing, and a nice thing at that, but the danger to our food supply is truly alarming. The question is, are we able to feed the world using holistic and sustainable means? Organic farming methods are now claimed by many to produce similar yields to intensive methods and use a third less energy, less water and no pesticides. Organic farms are also diversified, with many different crops, to avoid huge monocultures.

More people are voting with their feet when shopping in supermarkets by buying organic and free-range produce, others are becoming beekeepers, even in rooftops in cities. Apart from being a fulfilling hobby, beekeeping should also ensure a supply of increasingly precious honey, which could then be sold. We can also ensure that we create suitable habitats in our gardens for bees, by planting suitable flowering plants. By taking care of bees, we take care of ourselves – in fact, our lives could depend on the humble bumble bee.

the remaining resources become increasingly diminished very rapidly, due to the power of the 'essential exponential'.

This inexorable consequence causes Professor Bartlett to question some of the experts' opinions that we have sufficient oil reserves for a few hundred years or more and coal reserves for thousands of years. These estimates appear optimistic if

we consider the steadily increased rate of depletion, due to population growth at the very least – an increase of just a few per cent leads to a reverse geometric progression, such as Malthus was using to analyse population growth. A simple example is the myth of the ancient Persian king who was so delighted with the inventor of the game of chess, that he asked his subject what he wanted as a reward. The subject replied that he would like a single grain of rice on the first square of the chessboard and then the grains of rice to be doubled on each successive square of the board – a trifling amount, thought the king. The amount of rice on each square would be 1, 2, 4, 8, 16, 32, 64 and so on, and as there are sixty-four squares on the board, he would end up with around four times the annual global rice production of today – many, many billions of grains of rice! The depletion of resources works the other way around, obviously.

The United Nations' population statistics estimate that the world population in 2010 is around seven billion, and they think that it will increase to about nine billion by 2050. As they are making projections so far into the future, they give a wider range a few centuries from now, the mid-range of which is a stabilization of world population at around ten billion by 2300. This is based, possibly somewhat optimistically, on a lowering of the rate of fertility and generally ageing populations. However, they also show high and low scenarios, with the highest scenario continuing at an exponential rate, and an even higher exponential rate at worst.

At some point we reach the biological carrying capacity of the planet or run out of non-renewable resources, if we are not able to find sustainable solutions, almost regardless of climate change and global warming. One of Professor Bartlett's 'laws of sustainability' states that the size of the population that can be sustained (the carrying capacity) and the average standard of living of the population, are inversely related to one another. A circular, rather than linear, approach to resources, which eliminates the concept of waste, seems desirable to say the least. Or those *Mad Max* movies may turn out as documentaries of the future, after all!

SUSTAINABLE DEVELOPMENT

Ban-Ki-Moon, the United Nations Secretary-General, used the analogy that 'Our foot is on the gas pedal, and it is time we took it off... we must stop this from happening further' when describing the loss of Arctic sea ice as happening at a rate that was thirty years ahead of the predicted 'schedule' in 2009. He went on to state that 'Unless we fight climate change, unless we stop this trend, we'll have devastating consequences for humanity'. The trend has a long history, and it would be remiss of me not to include the famous Brundtland definition of sustainable development that we still aspire to, over two decades after its formulation in 1987: 'Sustainable development is development that meets the needs of the present without compromising the ability of future generations to meet their own needs'.

The past may be a foreign country but the future is an unknown continent. The Stern Report was commissioned by the UK Government's Treasury Department and published in 2005 – surprisingly for a definitive economic analysis of climate change, it contains at least one concession to dark humour amongst its several hundred pages, 650-odd pages in: 'we apply only a low discounting rate to the future simply because it is the future (we account for the possibility of extinction)'. Less humour is present in the pronouncement that there could be 'irreversible effects on future generations. It is as though a grandparent is saying to their grandchild, because you will live your life fifty years after mine, I place far less value on your well-being than I do on myself and my current neighbours, and therefore I am ready to take decisions with severe and irreversible implications for you.' A core purpose of the Stern Report was to devise a market in carbon with globally agreed social costs for carbon – the idea is that with an efficient market, carbon use should also be efficient.

In economic terms, the concept of the 'polluter pays' and consideration of the so-called 'externalities' of economic activities is gaining more mileage – although the idea that economic growth should be reduced by considerations of environment or ecology is probably still a bridge too far. However, interesting shifts in thought, such as those of prominent economist Herman Daly, could provide some solutions. Daly contends that 'Value added by labour and capital to natural resources is what we want to encourage, so don't tax it. Depletion and pollution (resource throughput) is basically a cost to be minimized so tax it.' This would have the effect of making natural resources more expensive at the point of extraction, with the effect that raw materials were more valuable, so that efficiency, maintenance and recycling is encouraged.

Professor Al Bartlett, and many others, including the UN now, put population growth right at the centre of the sustainability debate. Bartlett posits several 'laws of sustainability', of which the seventeenth and final one is that 'extinction is forever!' Fortunately, he has leavened his canons with some injections of humour, albeit rather dark, such as the sixteenth law, which alludes to the fact that the addition of the word 'sustainable' to our vocabulary, reports and institutions and so on is unlikely to guarantee that our existence becomes sustainable. However, his first law is possibly the most telling and is presumably in that position for that reason: 'Population growth and/or growth in the rates of consumption of resources cannot be sustained'; which does at least focus the mind on quite what it is that we are trying to sustain, when we keep using the word 'sustainable', very often gratuitously.

SUSTAINABLE HOUSING

Overview

The housing stock in the UK emits 25 per cent of our total carbon dioxide emissions, extending to 50 per cent if we include the entire built environment. The journey towards a low carbon or zero-carbon housing stock is one that we started some decades ago, during the oil shocks of the 1970s. The ultimate destination was delayed by an era of cheap energy, but now we have added an urgent environmental imperative to encourage us to continue this journey, and reach the right destination quickly. The economic and political circumstances that caused the energy crisis of the 1970s, triggered an almost unprecedented exploration into more efficient ways of living in our houses – resulting in a spate of passive solar dwellings, particularly in the sunnier regions of the world, not to mention the quest for the autonomous house.

Energy Efficiency

The buzz word back in the 1970s was 'energy con-servation', which gradually became energy effi-ciency, now replaced by sustainability. The wide applicability of the latter terms seems to have resulted in some woolly thinking at times, and a great deal of tokenism, which now attracts the dis-paraging term 'eco-bling' – such as small wind tur-bines mounted on the roofs of suburban houses,

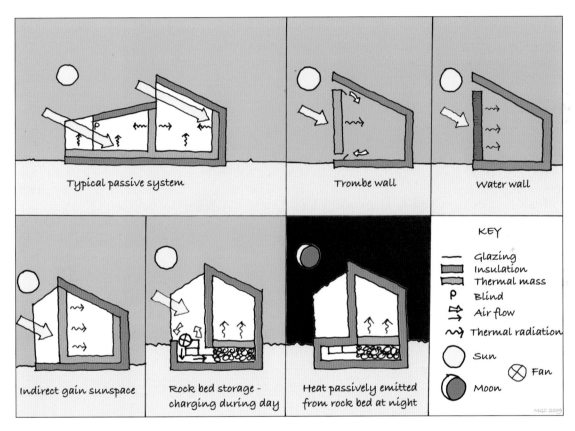

Passive solar design principles.

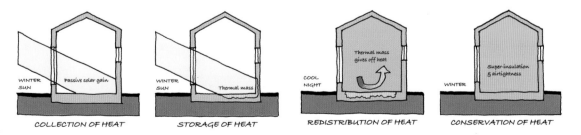

Solar heating principles.

sometimes occupied by politicians. There is rarely sufficient wind speed in such sheltered locations to make the investment in a small wind turbine ever pay off. Solar thermal and photo-voltaics are better investments in such locations, if the quest is for expensive 'eco-bling' and symbolism alone. Green roofs and walls should also be part of an integrated approach. A far more holistic approach is necessary in our existing and new housing stock, which begins with the basics that reduce energy demand and increase energy efficiency.

The basics of reducing energy demand can be very basic, and not nearly as exciting as installing arrays of photo-voltaics on your roof, but the no-

ABOVE: **Green wall.**

BELOW: **Embodied energy of insulation materials.**

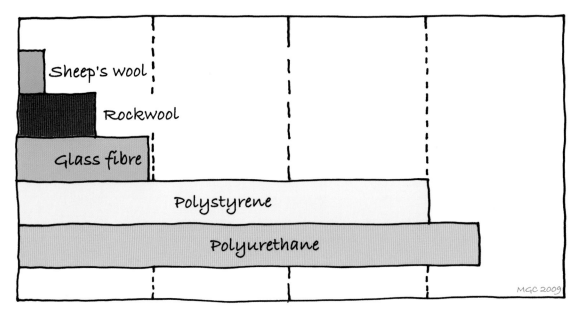

The Gaia Theory

The Gaia theory is named after the Greek earth goddess, and proposes that the planet's biosphere is a complex, holistic and interrelated system – like a single living organism. This ecological hypothesis was first mooted by James Lovelock and published as a paper in 1974, co-authored with biologist Lynne Margulis. Their ideas that the planet is a self-regulating system, with physics, chemistry, biology and humanity comprising a homogenous living system, is now an accepted theory, not to mention a branch of earth science. The author William Golding suggested the name, as the ancient Greeks also felt that the earth was a living being, and now modern science has rediscovered this theory.

Gaia theory states that all living things affect the earth's environment and provide feedback for potential equilibrium, rather like the theory that the flap of a butterfly's wing can cause untold effects on the other side of the world – the whole is greater than the sum of the parts. Lovelock hopes that the theory provides an appropriate framework for interdisciplinary work. He also cites the first images of the earth from space as the beginning of environmentalism and a more holistic view than objective scientific data. The latter show that Planet Earth is roughly the same size and made of the same elements as Mars and Venus, but they are dead planets. It seems more than random accident that our environment affords us protection against the hostile cold and radiation of outer space, with just the right constituent gases to allow life.

The proportion of oxygen has remained at nearly 20 per cent in the earth's atmosphere for millions of years. Ocean alkalinity, temperature and other environmental factors are also regulated by life. Temperature has remained within a very narrow range suitable for life on earth, despite the fact that the sun has increased its radiance and its potential to heat the earth by almost a third within the history of life. Such conditions are controlled by complex systems that we do not fully understand – it is more likely that we are a small part of a much larger whole, and as unnecessary for its continued existence as many of the species that we have made extinct. The Gaia theory is a useful device for us to examine our continuing actions.

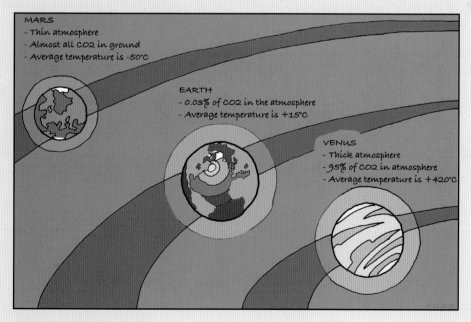

Three very different planets.

cost and low-cost measures are at least precisely that – inexpensive. The average house in the UK emits several tonnes of carbon dioxide each year, and half of that is probably in the heating. Aside from the most mundane of behavioural aspects, such as switching the lights off, installing energy efficient bulbs and turning appliances off at the mains rather than leaving them on stand-by (it is cheaper for the manufacturers to make them guzzle electricity on stand-by and pass the running costs on to you), super-insulating the loft with a benign material is probably your first priority in an existing house.

The UK Government has set a target of zero carbon for all new homes by 2016. This is an ambitious target, to say the least, but new homes are only a small percentage of the total housing stock, a few per cent. The vast majority of the housing stock we have now will still be with us in 2050. Ultimately, they must become zero carbon as well, or as close as possible – and it is possible to reduce the energy demand of old houses dramatically. Efficient housing stock is one thing, but how we use our houses is another, and behavioural aspects are equally important. Smart metering with inexpensive devices is a good way to monitor and control your electricity use, and save money with increased energy prices.

Simple energy efficiency measures received a fillip recently by dint of some research undertaken at the Grantham Institute for Climate Change at Imperial College London. Dr Adam Hawkes undertook a study that analysed several years of UK National Grid energy generation, to investigate the suitability of the average carbon dioxide emission factor used by the UK Government for policy purposes ('Estimating marginal CO_2 emissions rates for national electricity systems' *Energy Policy*, 2010). The factor is 0.43kg of CO_2/kWh; gas generation is approximately 0.2kgCO_2/kWh, while coal is nearer 0.6kgCO_2/kWh – he estimates that this could be some 60 per cent lower than the rate observed between 2002 and 2009 (0.69kgCO_2/kWh). This implies that policy studies are underestimating the impact of people reducing their electricity use, and that simple reduction measures have a great deal more impact on CO_2 emissions. Conversely, any small increases in the amount of electricity we use

could also have a much larger impact than previously estimated. Either way, we need to reduce electricity use.

The fact that simple energy efficiency and reduction measures may have a markedly increased impact on carbon emissions should motivate us to switch lights off when not in use, and install energy-efficient lightbulbs. These may seem like small interventions on an individual scale but it obviously adds up, and if everyone did it we could reduce the UK's carbon dioxide emissions by a third. Such basic lifestyle changes could remove the demand for about ten large gas-fired power stations. Reductions in energy demand allow only the more efficient power stations to supply electricity, rather than the older coal-fired ones, which are more carbon-intense (electricity has about two-and-a-half times the carbon impact of gas-fired equivalents, such as space heating).

Simple measures in each household, such as turning all appliances off at the mains when going to bed or going on holiday, would save around 100kgCO_2/year; installing ten energy-efficient lightbulbs would save up to 350kgCO_2/year; and hanging wet washing out to dry rather than using a tumble drier would save about 260kgCO_2/year. If all households took such measures we could reduce our carbon dioxide emissions by the equivalent of several million houses – a third of all houses. The UK Government response to Dr Hawke's report was that Britons need to wean themselves off fossil fuels and that inaction is not an option, as the cheapest way to cut carbon dioxide emission is through energy-saving measures – curbing energy waste and saving money.

New Housing

The aspiration for zero-carbon new housing by 2016 in the UK is challenging to say the least, and will require strategic housing supply decisions, as well as appropriate occupant behaviours. The building materials used in new zero-carbon houses present their own dilemmas, such as the provision of adequate thermal mass to absorb summertime heat, which may increase with global warming and climate change. Heavyweight materials usually supply more thermal mass than lightweight ones, but

ABOVE: **Heavyweight construction materials.**   BELOW: **Lightweight construction materials.**

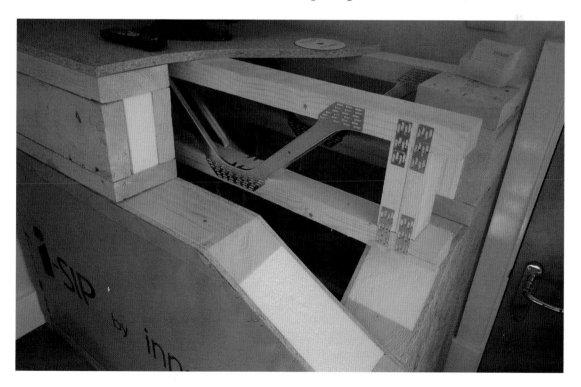

TOP LEFT: **Hempcrete solid wall construction.**

TOP RIGHT: **Limecrete block construction.**

BELOW: **Mechanical ventilation with heat recovery unit in a house.**

are usually more energy- and carbon-intensive in their manufacture (embodied energy) than light-weight ones, such as timber. However, new materials such as Hempcrete and Limecrete are emerging that give high thermal mass for houses in a sustainable fashion. Similar dilemmas exist with the advocacy of mechanical ventilation with heat recovery (MVHR) and reliance on natural ventilation in new zero-carbon houses – the former should allow for less heat loss from heating in winter, but needs good design and construction standards to ensure minimal thermal bridges and airtightness of the building envelope.

CONTRACTION AND CONVERGENCE

A Gigawatt (GW) is a billion watts (1,000,000,000W), which is the amount of energy that a large coal-fired power station, or large hydro-power scheme, or large nuclear plant generates in a year. A Terawatt (TW) is a GW × 1,000 –

humanity is currently using about 16TW of energy a year, with most of it coming from fossil fuels. This is the equivalent of 160 billion 100W lightbulbs burning all the time, emitting carbon dioxide into the atmosphere. It is technically possible for us to reduce our fossil fuel by 80 per cent in a few decades, so that carbon dioxide levels remain at 450 parts per million (ppm) – but is it politically possible?

Contraction and convergence is a proposed global framework that purports to secure human survival, by reducing greenhouse gas emissions to combat climate change in a socially equitable manner. C&C, as it is known in short, is the brainchild of a musician called Aubrey Meyer. He cites inspiration from watching a UK Channel Four television news broadcast in 1990, in which the five main global greenhouse gas polluters were listed as the USA, the (now former) USSR, China, India and Brazil. He was astounded that a nation such as India, a developing nation, could be listed in the same breath as large industrialized countries such

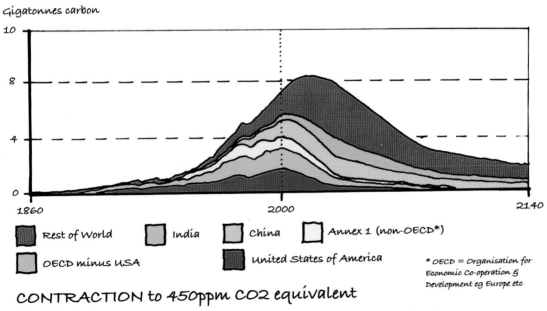

CONTRACTION to 450ppm CO2 equivalent

CONVERGENCE to equal per capita emissions at 2030

Contraction and convergence.

23

as America and Russia. At that time, per capita energy use in the USA was about twenty times that of India.

Meyer began to create the CGI (Global Commons Institute) with three friends from the British Green Party in 1990 – they included an ecologist, a science journalist and an IT specialist, who brought a wider range of skills to the endeavour. They started from the consensus that social justice demanded equal rights to the limited natural resources of the earth, for all its inhabitants. They also adopted the precautionary principle from the Kyoto Protocol (1992) – Article 3.3 states that signing parties should take precautionary measures to anticipate, prevent or minimize the causes of climate change and mitigate its adverse effects. Where there are threats of serious or irreversible damage, lack of full scientific certainty should not be used as a reason for postponing such measures.

Contraction and convergence is based on the idea of the rich, developed nations reducing their carbon dioxide emissions at a faster rate, while allowing the developing countries to continue industrialization and development until they reach comparable levels of development. The developed nations have caused most of the present carbon dioxide emissions in the atmosphere – and enjoyed the concomitant benefits of economic prosperity and growth. Conversely, the developing poor nations are usually the ones who will suffer the effects of climate change the most – because of their geographic locations they will be susceptible to sea-level rises and other potential ecological catastrophes and disasters.

The C&C framework is deliberately flexible about the target level of carbon dioxide in the atmosphere and the timing for convergence to reach that level. However, it is generally agreed that levels of between 350 to 450ppm by volume of carbon dioxide in the atmosphere are safe levels. C&C aims to meet those safe levels by 2140 in a natural manner. To reach such targets for the United Kingdom, the population would have to cut their personal carbon dioxide emissions by about 60 to 90 per cent, while other poorer developing nations would be given far less stringent

The Centre for Alternative Technology (CAT) was founded in an abandoned slate quarry in mid-Wales nearly four decades ago, ironically by a businessman. Old Etonian Gerald Morgan-Grenville was perplexed at the notion that humanity was living far beyond its earthly means. As the threat of potential ecological disaster becomes more real, CAT is rapidly becoming more of a mainstream organization – a far cry from its founder's inspiration as he travelled around the world exploring counter-culture and hippy communities that were pioneering self-sufficiency and autonomous ways of living. He decided that a research centre was necessary to address the problem and bought a disused slate quarry near Machynlleth in mid-Wales. His vision was initially supported by volunteers.

CAT's original mission, on the cusp of the end of the Cold War, and in the midst of the energy crisis of the 1970s, was to train people how to survive a post-apocalyptic future – a dearth of

Funicular railway at the entrance to CAT.

CAT Sharpens its Claws

Photovoltaic installation at CAT.

to use sustainable materials and technology, in order to promote their wider use in the construction industry, such as rammed earth walls. Rammed earth has a similar thermal mass to concrete, but with much lower environmental impact – constructed with successive layers of earth, which are then compacted, it gives a pleasant appearance without any decorative finish. Hempcrete is also used in the new building – another low-embodied energy material made from hemp stalks, lime and a small amount of cement. The thick Hempcrete walls provide good insulation and airtightness with good breathability – the walls are finished with a traditional and historic coat of naturally yellow lime render.

natural resources. Although this suggests a survivalist mentality, the Centre was always highly accessible to the public, so that it could disseminate and fund its research. Displays have gradually evolved over the decades, in what were then highly esoteric areas of renewable energy generation, recycling and sustainable methods of building design and construction. Small beginnings now boast a staff of nearly a hundred and postgraduate courses for building professionals, as well as short courses for renewable-energy installers and members of the general public.

CAT's educational activities were recently given a boost by the WISE building (Wales Institute for Sustainable Education), which includes en suite study bedrooms, teaching spaces and a lecture theatre. The new building provided an opportunity

Accommodation wing of the WISE building at CAT.

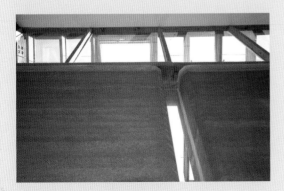

Rammed earth construction at CAT.

CAT's mission is to disseminate ways of understanding and working with nature, rather than trying to overcome it. The displays are intended to show people the impact they have on the environment and help them to find ways of reducing this impact – from the dramatic whole-house approach to smaller initial interventions. Their mission statement includes instilling the desire to change by practical example; providing the most appropriate information; and providing continuing support to put the change into practice. Whatever stage you are at on the journey to zero carbon, a day out at CAT never fails to inspire, inform and help you to get closer to the destination.

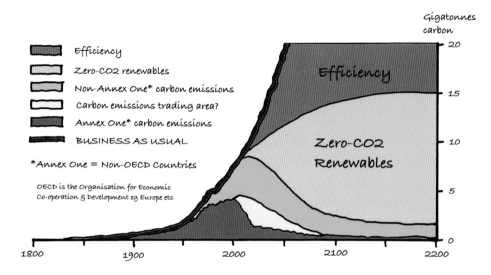

Gigatonnes
carbon

Contraction and convergence – how it could work.

Legend:
- Efficiency
- Zero-CO2 renewables
- Non-Annex One* carbon emissions
- Carbon emissions trading area?
- Annex One* carbon emissions
- BUSINESS AS USUAL

*Annex One = Non-OECD Countries

OECD is the Organisation for Economic
Co-operation & Development eg Europe etc

targets. The contraction part of C&C relates to the reduction of the total amount of carbon dioxide being put into the atmosphere. The convergence part of the framework deals with the entitlements to emit carbon dioxide and their distribution between countries of the world. Support for the C&C framework includes the UN, RIBA and renowned environmental campaigner George Monbiot.

CHAPTER SUMMARY

- Climate change is the biggest threat that our civilization has ever had to face, according to Professor Sir David King, the former Chief Scientific Advisor to the UK Government.
- The recent climate conference in Copenhagen did not produce a global protocol, but 150 heads of states produced a document that takes us forward. Developing countries, such as Indonesia, have committed to reduce their carbon emissions by 26 per cent; Brazil said that they will stop all deforestation and start reforestation by 2025 – and a large part of our rising carbon dioxide emissions are from deforestation.
- The world's population is now doubling every forty years, has reached seven billion, and is set

to rise to nearly ten billion by 2100 or earlier. The last two centuries of this extraordinary progress and growth were fuelled by fossil fuels.
- We are currently over-fishing our oceans. Large-scale industrial fishing began in about 1950, with the result that experts estimate that the once relative abundance of large fish is now reduced by about 90 per cent. Experts predict that, if current trends are allowed to continue, stocks of fish that we now eat could collapse by 2050.
- Thomas Malthus (1766–1834) thought that the dangers of population growth would preclude endless progress. He thought that the increase of population is necessarily limited by the earth's means of subsistence. Malthus cited the geometric or exponential progression of population growth, contrasted with the arithmetic or straight-line growth of the means of subsistence or food supply. A reverse exponential curve could apply to our rapid depletion of these resources, particular as population growth continues to explode.
- Professor Al Bartlett points to what he calls the 'essential exponential', the geometric progression – if our use of finite resources, such as oil and coal, increases by even a small percentage year-on-year, the remaining resources become

increasingly diminished very rapidly, due to the power of the 'essential exponential'.

- Honeybees are in decline due to intensive agriculture, pesticides, loss of habitat and human invention to increase their productivity. They are an indicator species and their demise should serve as a warning, as a third of our diet depends on their activities. Other species have suffered decline and extinction due to human interventions and environmental pollution. Organic farming is more sustainable and produces good yields in many cases.

- Sustainable development demands a circular, rather than linear, approach to resources, which eliminates the concept of waste. Sustainable development is development that meets the needs of the present without compromising the ability of future generations to meet their own needs. Shifting taxation burdens to nearer the point of extraction of natural resources, so that depletion and pollution are minimized, is one way of encouraging efficiency and recycling.

- Professor Al Bartlett's first law of sustainability is that 'Population growth and/or growth in the rates of consumption of resources cannot be sustained'. His final one is that 'extinction is forever!'

- UK housing stock emits 25 per cent of our total carbon dioxide emissions. The journey towards a low carbon or zero-carbon housing stock is one that we started some decades ago, during the oil shocks of the 1970s – we need to continue that journey to its ultimate destination.

- Energy efficiency is the obvious starting point, followed by holistic interventions rather than the addition of eco-bling to houses. Behavioural aspects, such as switching the lights off, installing energy-efficient bulbs and turning appliances off at the mains rather than leaving them on stand-by, are also important. Smart metering is a good way to monitor and control your electricity use.

- Simple energy-efficiency measures are more effective than previously accounted for, as the carbon dioxide emission factor of $0.69kgCO_2/$kWh should be used for electricity savings, rather than $0.43kg\ CO_2/kWh$. This means that simple electricity reductions are up to 60 per cent more effective than previously thought in the UK. If all households took such measures, we could reduce our carbon dioxide emissions by the equivalent of several million houses – a third of all houses.

- The Gaia theory proposes that the planet's biosphere is a complex, holistic and interrelated system, like a single, living organism. Gaia theory states that all living things affect the earth's environment and provide feedback for potential equilibrium – the whole is greater than the sum of the parts.

- The aspiration for zero-carbon new housing by 2016 in the UK is challenging. Thermal mass in building fabric absorbs summertime heat, which may increase with global warming and climate change. New materials, such as Hempcrete and Limecrete, are emerging that give high thermal mass for houses in a sustainable fashion.

- Contraction and convergence is a proposed global framework for reducing greenhouse gas emissions to combat climate change in a socially equitable manner. C&C is based on the idea of the rich, developed nations reducing their carbon dioxide emissions at a faster rate, while allowing the developing countries to continue industrialization and development until they reach comparable levels of development. It aims to reduce carbon dioxide levels in the atmosphere to safe levels by 2140, in a natural manner.

- The Centre for Alternative Technology (CAT) was founded in an abandoned slate quarry in mid-Wales in the 1970s. CAT's mission is to educate and train people to live in a sustainable manner. They disseminate ways of understanding and working with nature, rather than trying to overcome it.

CHAPTER 2

Evolutionary Houses

The principal objective of the project is to devise a house which can be independent of mains' services and might therefore be located ... anywhere in the world. The use of ambient energy implies a house with low-energy demand, which can be provided by both passive and active means.

Alexander Pike, RIBA (1978)

EARLY DEVELOPMENTS

Autonomy and self-sufficiency in houses is hardly revolutionary, as we have used renewable sources of energy, such as the sun and log fires, for centuries – millennia, even, if you include our time in caves back to the discovery of fire. In more recent times, the Roman architect and military engineer Marco Polio Vitruvius, advocated orienting houses to the south to benefit from passive solar energy, particularly for the warming effect of the sun in the depths of winter. He even prescribed the displacement of rooms to take advantage of the path of the sun throughout the day, such as bedrooms and kitchens facing east to take advantage of the rising sun. In medieval times, we called the lounge or sitting-room the 'solar', which gives some clue as to the room's orientation – for daylight and warmth.

Solar energy influenced urban planning and house design until the discovery of electricity a century or so ago. A widespread use of renewable energy was obviously necessary before that and there were experiments to drive engines and pumps by focusing sunlight in the late nineteenth century. Flat-plate solar collectors were used in California for domestic hot water in the early twentieth century. Since then many efforts to use solar and other renewable energy sources in house

design were made. Research and development was intensified in the 1970s due to the global oil shocks, and as non-renewable energy sources are further depleted, alternatives become more and more cost-effective. Serious attempts to design the autonomous or zero-carbon house probably start with the Dymaxion House by Buckminster Fuller in the first half of the twentieth century.

DYMAXION HOUSE
Dynamic Maximum Tension
The evolution of attempts at zero-carbon houses, or at least autonomous or self-sufficient dwellings, stretches back many decades, at least until the middle of the twentieth century, if not earlier in isolated examples. The radical American architect and futurist visionary Buckminster Fuller, developer of the geodesic dome, is often cited as conceiving of the forerunner of the zero-carbon house in his Dymaxion Houses (Dymaxion is a shortening of Dynamic Maximum + ion, as in 'tension', for example). The first of these was completed in the late 1920s and featured a hexagonal floor plan, with a distinctively triangular organizational grid – an exhibition catalogue to advertise the concept was laid out in a triangular design format, even the text, and labelled the 'Minimum Dymaxion House'.

Fuller was directing an uncompromising assault on domestic architecture, and taking the Swiss architect Le Corbusier's 1923 architectural manifesto in *Vers une Architecture* to its relentlessly logical and efficient conclusion – what if the house was really 'a machine for living in', that could be efficiently mass-produced like an automobile or any other industrial product, and also operate with maximum, machine-like efficiency?

4-D Prefabricated House

Fuller engaged in a tenacious round of lectures and publicity in his attempts to push the early Dymaxion House, or 4-D House as it was originally called (the fourth dimension was time), dressed in a dark suit and tie like a travelling salesman, with various demonstration-scaled models of the house, which packed down into a suitcase – putting the salesman's sample case to a new and ironic use. The early house was designed for construction with the latest lightweight metal and aluminium alloys (e.g. Duralumin), so that it could be transported by Zeppelin and 'landed' anywhere in the country or the world. Ideally, the Zeppelin would simply drop a bomb on the designated site, in order to excavate the ground for the foundations of the single, central, supporting column, which contained all of the environmental services and plumbing. There was even a ten-storey example – an autonomous and self-sufficient dwelling that was lightweight, portable, energy efficient, self-ventilating, self-temperature regulating and self-cleaning.

Somewhat prescient of the internet, Fuller envisaged that the intricate communication module at the centre of the dwelling, which included a library, globe, maps, drawing board, typewriter, mimeograph, phonograph, telephone, radio and television, would reconnect the self-sufficient home to the world whose physical infrastructure it floated above like a flying saucer. His manifesto for the Dymaxion House included the aspiration that the house should eliminate drudgery, exploitation, selfishness, politics and centralized control; safeguard against flood, electrical storms, fire, earthquakes, tornadoes, hurricanes and marauders; and save time for education, amusement and advancement. All of which should be the real objectives for architects and architecture, in his view, rather than aesthetic concerns – although Fuller saw the proposals as not about architecture, but rather a scientific experiment for the benefit of all humanity – a benign revolution in mass-market housing.

Dymaxion 'Wichita' House

The original Dymaxion House did not take off commercially, but the Dymaxion Deployment Unit or DDU, which was inspired by cheap, corrugated steel grain bins, adapted into temporary accommodation units, was manufactured at the rate of 1,000 units a day during the Second World War. Most of them ended up in the Middle East for use as transit aircrew accommodation – the remarkable natural ventilation system, using a central roof extractor, allegedly allowed it to remain cool in hot climates. The ultimate Dymaxion House was initially called the Dymaxion House II, but was quickly renamed the Dymaxion Dwelling Machine or Wichita House, after the place in Kansas where it was built. Fuller Houses Incorporated was set up to mass produce the houses in an aeroplane factory, in order to turn the war effort into the peace effort and to provide economic accommodation for returning heroes.

Production of the Wichita House, autonomous dwelling units, was helped by the order for two prototypes by the US Army Air Corps. They were circular in plan with a central, hollow stainless steel column that housed utilities and plumbing, supported on a single foundation, with radiating floor beams and a tensile structure, like the spokes of a bicycle wheel, supporting the roof from the central column. Construction was facilitated by the central structural column, which was used to winch the roof up, once it was assembled on the floor. They were clad with aluminium sheeting with a shallow, dome-shaped roof, which created a ventilation effect that sucked cooler air downwards when vented properly. The aerodynamic ventilator at the top of the structure pivoted from the central column to act as a wind-catcher to catch cool breezes and to circulate air to the interior. It also rendered the dwelling tornado-proof.

29

Buckminster Fuller – the Planet's Altruistic Genius

Richard Buckminster Fuller (1895–1983).

Buckminster Fuller's wider geometric theories are contained in his 1975 publication *Synergentics*, which expounds on his thesis of space being tetrahedral (triangular) – evidenced by his architectural proposals being based on geometry using triangles, circles and tetrahedrons, rather than conventional architectural geometries of planes and rectangles. He is most famously known for the geodesic dome, which combines the sphere, as the most efficient volume container, with the tetrahedron, which gives the most efficient structural strength-to-weight ratio. Fuller was awarded US patents and developed the concept in the 1950s.

The geodesic dome is the only structure that gets stronger and lighter in density with size – some 300,000 geodesic domes are built worldaround (as Fuller would say: worldwide is a flatearth term). Famous geodesic domes include the Biosphere at the Montreal Expo in 1967, Spaceship Earth at Disney World in Florida and the Eden Centre in Cornwall. Among his wilder ideas was that of enclosing Manhattan in a twomile wide, climate-controlled geodesic dome – it would apparently pay for itself in ten years from snow-clearance savings alone.

Richard Buckminster Fuller was born in Milton, Massachusetts in 1895 and expelled twice from Harvard for excessive socializing and missing his mid-term exams – he did not graduate. Bankrupted in his early thirties after an unsuccessful building business venture with his father-in-law, he began drinking heavily for a spell and contemplated suicide. The death of his young invalid daughter in 1922, from influenza, proved the catalyst for him to embark on 'an experiment to discover what the little, penniless, unknown individual might be able to do effectively on behalf of all humanity'. He blamed himself for his daughter's death, as he felt it was due to damp housing conditions, which caused him to focus on improving mass housing conditions for much of his career.

Such idealistic and altruistic aims were not always easy to fulfil – although he was not formally trained as an architect, many of his ideas involved the built environment and eventually found an audience in that realm. But it was not always so, as when he proffered the intellectual property rights for a crude forerunner of the Dymaxion House (the 4-D prefabricated house) to the American Institute of Architects in 1928 – the AIA were 'inherently opposed to any such pea-in-a-pod-like reproducible designs'. Fuller was finally awarded the AIA Gold Medal in 1970.

Fuller was an early environmental activist and coined the phrase 'emphemeralization' to mean 'doing more with less' – something we would do well to remember as a definition when we use the word 'sustainability'. He also popularized the term 'Spaceship Earth' and agreed with Francois de Chardenede's view that oil, representing as it does the product of millions of years of incoming solar flux, or ancient sunlight, is an expensive commodity to use to commute to work – at around, effectively, over a million dollars a gallon. Ironically, Fuller was a frequent flier who eccentrically wore three watches: one each for the current, last and future time-zones that he was flying through, from and to. Famously, he said that the most important fact about Spaceship Earth is that it did not come with a manual.

Fuller's early mission to change the world for good is fulfilled by his legacy of ideas and inventions, documented in thirty publications and rewarded with many honorary doctorates from universities around the world. Further new words he coined include 'livingry' (as opposed to weaponry), and 'sunsight' and 'sunclipse' to replace the earth-centric terms of sunrise and sunset. As an eternal optimist, Fuller felt that humanity had transcended warfare, as cooperation was the optimum survival strategy. In a fitting and apt tribute, considering our current concern with carbon, a new carbon molecule, which resembles the shape of a geodesic dome, was named a Buckminsterfullerine, commonly known as a 'Fuller Ball'. He died in 1983 at the age of 88, within hours of his wife. In the lines of the recent rock song, 'Buckminster Fuller we need you now'.

Dymaxion 'Wichita House': ground-floor plan, 1947.

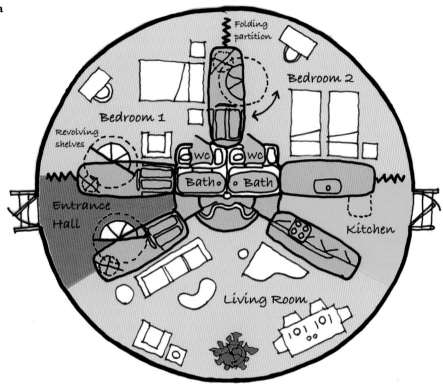

The Wichita House included an autonomous toilet and water storage, which reduced water usage with a grey water system and a spray-mist shower to conserve water. The compactly designed interior contained circular, revolving storage facilities (with paternoster shelving) to save space and was about 90m^2 (1,000ft^2) in floor area, costing the equivalent of a top-end motor car, and half the price of a conventional house of the day. Ideally, they could be rented with a service-provision arrangement, rather like renting a telephone line. The Dymaxion bathroom was prefabricated in copper and alloys of tin, and apparently a joy to use – plastic versions of the bathroom were available into the 1980s. However, criticism of the house included its specific architectural design, which ignored context, and the high, embodied energy of its materials, such as aluminium – but this was a logical material choice to capitalize on post-war aircraft production capacity, and the house was intended for construction in former aircraft factories.

The Wichita House prototype provided occupants with filtered, natural ventilation, a fully fitted kitchen, two bathrooms, two bedrooms, integrated vacuum cleaner and movable partitions. Its external appearance was not dissimilar to an Airstream Trailer caravan, which still enjoys commercial success today, but it packed down into a stainless steel packing cylinder that was small and light enough for easy airlifting, and could be assembled in one day by a team of six. Sadly, the venture that could have revolutionized mass house production faltered, allegedly due to Fuller's perfectionism and desire to further develop the design before starting mass production. Fuller Houses Inc received about 37,000 orders for Wichita houses in a six-month period – the prototypes were purchased by a local businessman and lived in for many years, until its near-derelict remains were recovered by the Henry Ford Museum in 1992 and restored for display. One problem of rigid geometrical plans, such as circles, is the difficulty for extending the

DYMAXION HOUSE
Wichita House, 1946

MGC 2010

LEFT: **Dymaxion 'Wichita House', 1946.**

BELOW: **Whole House at CAT, Wales – view from the south.**

plan – the default owner got over this by using the parts of the second prototype to create a two-storey hybrid (he had six children).

Further development of the autonomous house was represented by a number of one-off experimental houses by MIT and others, usually in locations such as California to maximize solar collection, throughout the 1950s and 1960s. Buckminster Fuller largely concentrated on geodesic domes in the 1950s and 1960s, and there was a proposal for a 'geodesic autonomous living unit'

from this period – usually represented by a scale model of a fully-glazed geodesic dome, containing vegetation and a mezzanine living space. It was not until the oil crisis of the 1970s that an interest in resource-efficient habitation was rekindled. This included the creation of the Centre for Alternative Technology (CAT) in a disused slate quarry in mid-Wales, whose early experiments included what remains still the most heavily insulated house in Britain, and energy-efficient 'Segal Houses' (a low-cost, timber-framed, self-build housing approach, invented by the British architect, Walter Segal). But the work of this era is probably best symbolized by the work of a team of architects and engineers at Cambridge University, who started work on the Autarkic House in the early seventies.

TOP: **Whole House at CAT, Wales – showing wall insulation thickness.**

BELOW: **Walter Segal energy efficient house at CAT in mid-Wales.**

AUTARKIC HOUSE

Introduction

The fact that the autarkic house was born out of the white heat of technology, the space race and the landing of the first man on the moon in 1969 is evident from the architectural imagery the project finally came up with. There is no denying the fact that it does look like a spaceship or a NASA Apollo mission module that has just landed in a field, and if the aerogenerator, as the wind turbine was termed, was made to reverse the other way, it looks as if it could well take off again to land in another field, or indeed, on another planet.

The nomenclature of the project is something of a lexiconical saga in its own right, as it was originally called the autonomous housing project, with the intention that the scientifically resolved results would be mass produced and provide a solution to developing land that was remote from mains' services. It spawned many other contemporaneous attempts at autonomous houses, so that the project director Alexander Pike, in one of his reports in the late-1970s, changed the name to the autarkic house, to distance the project from what he felt were misguided copies. His use of the term autarkic was in the sense of complete self-sufficiency.

The Cambridge autarkic housing project was first conceived in the early 1970s, and pursued with some limited research grant budgets from the Science Research Council. This forced the team at Cambridge University School of Architecture to focus on occasional research papers, such as those written by now familiar names in the environmental architectural movement, such as Brenda and Robert Vale, and Randall Thomas. These research papers explored issues such as the solar heating and food production that would be necessary for a completely self-sufficient house for a family of three or four people. Typical titles were 'Results of solar collector study' and 'Land requirements and food production in an autonomous unit'.

This approach was explained as being necessary to make sure that the theoretical foundations for the autarkic house, and self-sufficient living, were fully explored, so that no meagre research resources were wasted in moving towards the building of an experimental house. The eventual

Autarkic House, 1978 – view from the south.

MGC 2010

**Autarkic House –
ground-floor plan.**

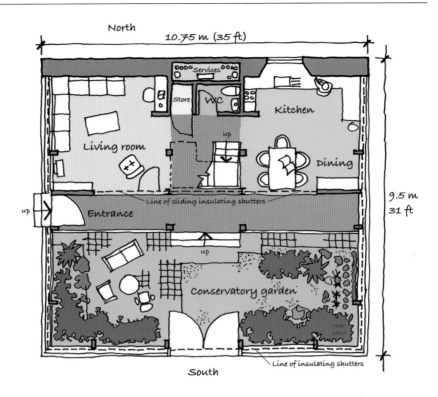

North

10.75 m (35 ft)

Services

Store

WC

Kitchen

up

Living room

Dining

++

Line of sliding insulating shutters

up

Entrance

9.5 m
31 ft

up

Conservatory garden

MGC 2010

Line of insulating shutters

South

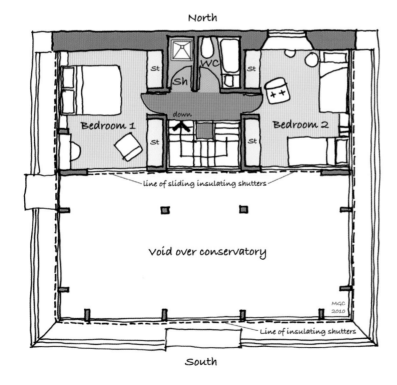

North

St

WC

St

Sh

++

down

Bedroom 1

Bedroom 2

St

St

line of sliding insulating shutters

Void over conservatory

MGC
2010

Line of insulating shutters

South

**Autarkic House –
first-floor plan.**

building of a prototype house was very much the intention from the start, and remained so even in the late-1970s, when a site on the outskirts of Cambridge was identified. The project had progressed to some firm proposals in the form of architectural drawings and specification, after several years of theoretical research, by the late-1970s. There is certainly no doubt that for future architectural practitioners, such as the Vales, who were architectural students at Cambridge at the time, the project provided a very pragmatic grounding for their later work on autonomous housing.

A constant theme of the project was the emphasis on providing appropriate or optimal environmental servicing of the house, to make it self-sufficient, which caused Randall Thomas to call the project an engineer's dream in a recent article. This is well illustrated by the precise and prosaic description of the food requirements, to provide 7,500kcal of energy to the family of three, who it was hoped would eventually live in the built demonstration house:

The recommended energy intake of 7,500kcal for, say, a typical family of three would need around 7,000m² (1.75 acres). Grain crops would be grown on 1,000m² (0.25 acres) and vegetables on 500m² (0.125 acres). Two goats and twelve hens would provide protein energy and variety in the diet, requiring about 4,100m² and 1,300m² (1.0 acres and 0.32 acres), respectively.

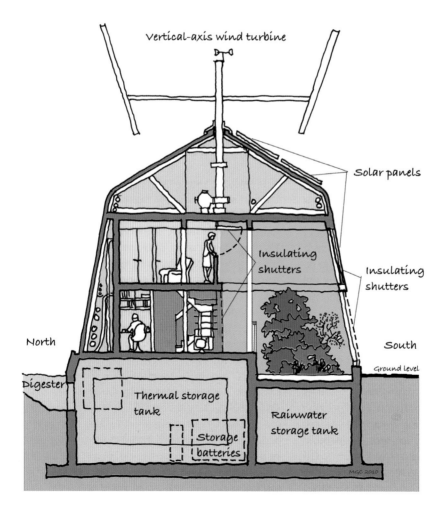

Autarkic House – cross-section.

Although undoubtedly providing sufficient nutrition for survival, there seems to be little scope in the dry specification for the odd trip to the supermarket for a pizza and a bottle of wine! Similar approaches were taken to other aspects of the project, which provided a good scientific grounding to what are often perceived as utopian proposals – precise calculations were also provided for energy and water supply and use. Early computer programs were developed and run to calculate these aspects to the last degree. The NASA space missions were inspirational for such a scientific approach to architectural survival – the sight of the blue-green orb of Plant Earth seen from space, for the first time, enabled us to perceive our existence in an entirely new perspective. Combined with the seemingly impending doom of an energy crisis, three-day week, oil price shocks and high rates of inflation, it is little surprise that the decade of the 1970s inspired some radical thinking about more efficient ways of living and sheltering.

One of the key concepts of the house was that, despite the large, glazed conservatory area, this would clearly not be used all year round, but would be a boon in summer. During the winter months, of inclement weather at least, the occupants would retreat into the core of the house, with the idea of sliding, insulating shutters, so that heat could be conserved in this area; these were clearly shown on the drawings. In spite of its somewhat space-age architectural imagery, looking at the plans and sections, not to mention the model, which apparently still resides in the board room of the Martin Centre in Cambridge over a quarter of a century later, the autarkic house looks like quite a pleasant way to live.

The large conservatory, presumably full of flowering and cropping vegetation, has parallels with other lower-tech approaches being pursued in the same era, such as the 'earthships' developed by the American architect Michael Reynolds in the New Mexico desert and elsewhere. The down-to-earth approach of the latter also proposes a way of dealing with the excessive waste of a consumer society, by reusing old tyres and plastic bottles in the architectural fabric of the earthship.

Both the high- and low-tech approaches are conceived from similar starting points of passive and active features, such as thermal mass and solar panels.

Objectives and Justification

The main objectives of the project were to devise an environmental servicing system for houses that reduced dependence on finite local resources, which were increasingly subject to price inflation in an era of oil shocks and energy crisis. A parallel objective was to obviate some of the utility networks (and their losses), which imposed constraints on planned development in rural areas. The theory was that the use of naturally occurring energy, water and food sources would allow the development of otherwise marginal land areas – creating cheaper land for housing production. The research was initiated in 1971 by Alexander Pike, an architect who was leading the Technical Research Division in the Department of Architecture at Cambridge University. Small research budgets were obtained from the Science Research Council and the Department for the Environment, together with some commercial sponsorship.

There was an intention that the theoretical research work into the feasibility of autonomous housing would eventually proceed to the building of a prototype autonomous house and design guide for autonomous housing, and that this would form the basis for a largely mass-produced autonomous housing system. Justification for the proposed project was stated as:

- The price of oil, gas, electricity and food may rise by about 15 per cent per annum for the next ten years, quadrupling the current rates.
- The demand for private space may increase by about 10 per cent per annum over the next thirty years to achieve a maximum of one acre.
- Normal working time may reduce by 5 per cent each year for the next decade, eventually resulting in a three-day working week.
- These trends may stimulate the desire for families to produce their own power, water and food on site, reduction the tendency to waste and consequently, to pollute.

Those readers old enough, or younger, keen students of history, will note the last point with wry amusement, but such ideas of human efficiency improvements and improving technology increasing leisure time were common parlance of the era. Not to mention early times, such as those of time-and-motion studies in the early decades of the nineteenth century, that were supposed to yield a utopian age of freedom from drudgery for humanity. Sadly for us, such fantasies are now consigned to the same place that other fanciful notions, such as the paperless office, now reside in.

Autonomous Systems

Examples of the autonomous provision of energy, such as essential electricity demand for lighting, were seen as best provided from the wind, particularly where wind speeds were greater during the part of the year with least daylight; while the large demand for domestic, low-temperature space heating was seen as best provided by solar radiation. The small, domestic energy demand that lay between these two extremes, for activities such as cooking, was best provided for from digestive gas. Calculations for the latter suggested that 1 to 1.5MWh/year of methane were required, which could be obtained from the cultivation of 0.2 hectares (0.5 acres) of typical garden crops, which would provide 40kg per hectare (350lb/acre) of dried green waste.

The digester to produce methane was required, anyway, for sewage treatment – although its volume is slightly increased by the green waste contribution from the proposed horticulture. Any heat needed to maintain the digester at the right temperature for methane gas production (about 30°C or 80°F) was minimized by super-insulation, and some heat is already produced by decomposition. Additionally, heat can also accrue from the adjacent long-term hot-water storage tank, also in the basement of the house – only about 3 per cent (40kWh), in the coldest period of winter, was envisaged as necessary. An algae tank was also planned, to help with tertiary waste treatment.

Electricity

As the project was investigated in the mid-1970s

long before the general advent of LED lighting, it envisaged largely tungsten electric lighting operating at low efficiency (1 to 5 per cent), possibly increased to 10–15 per cent efficiency with fluorescent tube lighting – but all-in-all, accounting for only a few per cent of the total domestic energy consumption. Gas lighting at an efficiency of around 3 per cent was not seen as a sustainable improvement on electricity, as it was no more abundant than wind power. As such, it was concluded that electricity for lighting was best supplied by wind generated power. This was relatively expensive for the first 1,200kWh/year, at four times the cost of the typical electricity mains price, even when taken from storage batteries – and including the wind-turbine mounting as part of the building. However, more than the 1,200kWh/year, drawn directly from the turbine, was roughly equal to the cost of mains supplied electricity.

Mechanical Power

Storing electrical power from the wind turbine in batteries was not always seen as the optimal strategy, as it was often more efficiently obtained directly from the rotor, particularly where the energy demand coincided with the occurrence of wind, i.e. random with slightly more required in winter. The site under consideration in Cambridgeshire experienced 60 per cent more wind energy in the winter months (October to March) than in the six summer months. Optimally, the wind turbine could be connected to a heat-pump compressor to increase the temperature in the long-term water store, or running the power supply directly in winter. Integrating the vertical-axis wind turbine into the building design was a way of ameliorating its costs, but it also led to additional structural and noise-insulation costs – set off against some increase in local wind speed to the blade caused by the proximity to the building form. Wind-tunnel tests were proposed for different building forms and shapes.

Heating

In the mid-1970s, with lower U-values (heat loss through a section of structure) for building fabric than today, it was estimated that space heating accounted for 70–80 per cent of all domestic energy requirements. Space heating used energy at a relatively low density (50–100W/m^2 of floor area) and temperature (15–30°C). As solar radiation is of a similar density (150W/m^2 continuous) and temperature range, it is the most appropriate energy source for space heating, also allowing for the use of inter-seasonal storage (using water as it has the highest specific heat capacity of all materials, giving it the ability to store the most heat per cubic unit) and a topping-up system.

Super-insulated building fabric standards were specified, which made ventilation heat losses more important. The desire for low rates of ventilation, to reduce heat loss, also focused attention on the potential contribution of oxygen (and reduction of carbon dioxide) from plant growth during the day (but the reverse would happen at night). They considered that the water-heating load was comfortably provided for by 40m^2 (430ft^2) of solar panels, throughout the year, even in England. The cost of this energy was estimated at about 1 pence per kWh, assuming 30 per cent efficiency of total insulation.

Water

Water supply autonomy was largely seen as achievable from rainwater collection and purification from gravity and sand filters. Even in the comparatively high rainfall area of Cambridge, minimum storage capacity was prescribed as 10m^3 (353ft^3), to allow for the possibility of intermittent drought conditions. The use of water in the long-term heat-storage tank gave an obvious source for emergency supply. However, the highest demand for water supplies coincides with the lowest rainfall in early summer – so solar distillation was considered a distinct possibility, as water purification, like space heating, also requires low-grade energy (such as solar radiation).

The team calculated that about 1.6ltr/m^2 (0.26 pints/ft^2) per day was obtainable in summer, from such secondary sources. The proposed solar still was integrated into the roof design, ideally sloping at 20 degrees. Reverse osmosis filtration was also considered, to augment recycled water flow. Various computer programs were developed for

Solar Still

A solar still is an alternative technological way of distilling water, powered by the heat of the sun. This way of obtaining water is often prescribed in survival courses, when a pit is dug and then covered with a plastic sheet, with a stone in the centre to depress the sheet into a conical shape – a water-collecting receptacle is placed underneath the plastic sheet. The heat and humidity of the soil and the relative cool of the plastic cause water to evaporate on to the cool surface of the plastic. In a solar still, contaminated water is excluded, outside the collector, where it is evaporated by the sun. The pure water vapour condenses on the cool, inner surface of the plastic sheet and drips off into the receptacle below the low, weighted point, where it is collected.

optimizing rainwater storage capacity, collection area and consumption patterns for given regimes of supply and purification. This has been coupled to a routine for simulating performance of the solar still under a range of variables.

Food

The necessary food and calorific intake required to sustain a typical family of three in the Autarkic House was scientifically calculated as 7,500kcal a day. Recommended calorie intakes, today, are estimate at 2,500kcal for an adult man and 2,000kcal for an adult woman or a teenager. But these are assuming a relatively sedentary lifestyle, such as a desk job with little or no exercise. No doubt the Autarkic House lifestyle would provide some moderate exercise, such as tending crops and livestock, which would justify an increase of at least 500kcal/day for the adult male and around 250kcal/day for the female and teenager! The team estimated that this level of nutritional energy would require about 7,000m^2 (1.75 acres) of land, and envisaged that grain crops would be grown on 1,000m^2 (0.25 acres), and vegetables on 500m^2 (0.125 acres). Livestock of two goats and twelve hens provided protein energy and diet variation, and they would require about 4,100m^2 and 1,300m^2 (1.0 acres and 0.32 acres), respectively.

Conclusions

The name Autarkic House was coined to distinguish the project from a range of projects using the term autonomous house throughout the decade of the 1970s. These other projects were perceived as exploiting ambient energy and recycling methods to supplement conventional systems. The Autarkic House was allegedly unique in its ambition to achieve complete self-sufficiency, with a fully integrated servicing system, so that it did not require any connection to mains' utilities. This was intended to allow it to be built anywhere, on marginal and remote land, rather in the tradition of Buckminster Fuller's ideas for the Dymaxion House.

Although the potential for virtually unlimited housing development is alarming in terms of low-density land use, the ambition avoids costly infrastructure and development patterns, such as urban sprawl and ribbon development (one house deep along roads), but might lead more to pepper-pot development (isolated rural dwellings). And it is unlikely, with exploding population growth (world population is now double what it was in 1970 – currently at 7 billion), that we have enough space on the globe to fill solely with independent autonomous houses – higher density solutions are probably required in the main, as the proportion of the population living in cities continues to increase. The lucky few live the 'good life' in the autonomous house.

The Cambridge team made much of the thorough theoretical underpinnings and scientific calculations they made, considering that other 'solutions' that were actually constructed were insufficiently monitored, so that their usefulness was compromised by the ignorance of their actual performance. The Autarkic House sought to design a house that was independent of mains' utilities so that it could be sited virtually anywhere in the world. Using ambient energy sources implied a dwelling with low energy demand that could be supplied by both passive and active means. The former include super-insulation of the building fabric, reduced space standards and controlled solar gain, while the latter covers heat recovery from the wind turbine and out-flowing warm air and water.

The project also proposed ways of achieving independence from mains' water supply and drainage by collecting rainwater, integrating waste-disposal systems and reducing domestic electrical energy needs and hot-water demand. The detailed monitoring of the performance of an inhabited prototype was intended as the final stage of the project, while the ultimate goal was that this would provide a design guide for the use of ambient and renewable energy sources in new and existing houses. It is a great shame that a prototype house was not built on the site provided by the University of Cambridge, just outside the city – the time is probably nigh for a reconsideration!

Summary

The Autarkic House was conceived as a completely self-sufficient dwelling with a compact shape (roughly a cube), with a super-insulated fabric, that tends to conserve energy – the large areas of glazing in the conservatory allowed passive solar gain and food cultivation. Space standards were quite basic in the 'inner core' of the house, but the separating insulated shutters were open to the conservatory for most of the year – only under extreme climatic conditions would they be closed to reduce heat losses. Construction was timber-framed with a central steel tower to support the wind turbine, and thermal mass provided from reinforced-concrete floors and partitions. The conservatory was double-glazed with triple-glazing for the windows of the house. A long-term thermal, storage, steel tank containing water, surrounded by polyurethane insulation was envisaged in a reinforced-concrete basement.

The energy demand of the house was reduced by using approaches such as heavy insulation, heat recovery on both exhaust air and waste water, special detailing to reduce air infiltration, water-saving spray taps and showers, fluorescent lighting tubes and a cold-water washing-machine. It was thought that these strategies would reduce the energy demand of the Autarkic House to less than a third of a contemporary detached house. This minimized energy demand was met by a solar collector system for space and domestic hot-water heating, and a wind turbine for electricity demand. The solar panels were seen as an integral part of the weathertight building envelope to reduce costs. Systems were integrated, where possible, to optimize energy and materials used; for example, excess electricity from the wind-turbine system was stored in the thermal store, and waste heat from the inverter contributed towards house heating. The environmental servicing system comprised of:

- Solar energy: a gravity-fed water system used the solar radiation incident on collectors on the roof and south wall to charge long-term storage tanks.
- Electricity supply: a vertical-axis wind turbine drove an alternator whose output was used to charge batteries. The batteries supplied power to a house through an inverter.

- Heating and ventilating: warm air flowing in ducts was used with hot water flowing in a loop to provide space heating. The system integrated both the solar energy and electrical supply circuits.
- Water supply: rainfall was stored and purified, as necessary. Water was recycled by a reverse osmosis unit when required. Waste hot-water preheated the cold-water supply, which was then increased to domestic hot-water temperatures from the long-term thermal storage tank.
- Waste disposal: an experimental sewage digester was installed but connection to mains' drainage was provided as an emergency backup.

AUTONOMOUS HOUSE

The Autonomous House was a far more memorable project title than the Autarkic House from this period, and the term was immortalized in the eponymous title of Robert and Brenda Vale's of the

Brenda and Robert Vale – autonomous house pioneers.

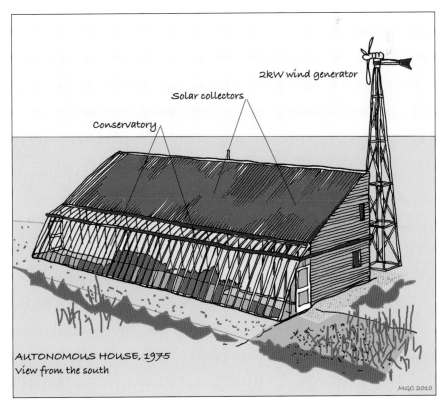

Autonomous House from the south, 1975 – Brenda and Robert Vale.

Conservatory

Solar collectors

2kW wind generator

AUTONOMOUS HOUSE, 1975
view from the south

MGC 2010

mid-1970s. *The Autonomous House: Designing and Planning for Self-Sufficiency* was published in 1975, and defined its subject as a 'house operating independently of any inputs except those of its immediate environment... not linked to the mains' services of gas, water, electricity or drainage... uses the income-energy sources of sun, wind and rain to service itself and process its own wastes'. The autonomous house book starts with a chapter that describes the philosophy of an appropriate technology approach, rather than technology for its own sake – this is aptly symbolized by the low-tech architecture illustrated on the cover (little more than a 'lean-to' in form and appearance with a wind turbine on a latticed tower), which is a model of the Autonomous House 1 proposal in the 1975 edition of the book.

The book includes a further seven chapters, which outline, in some detail, the appropriate technologies that make up an autonomous house proposal – running through power from the wind and sun, heat pumps, recycled waste, water, batteries and fuel cells, and storing heat. Architectural proposals, such as they are, are confined to a few pages in an appendix, in which 'The data assembled in the book have been used as the basis for the design of an autonomous house for a family of four, sited on a one-acre plot'. The entire preceding book resembles a performance specification for the possibilities of the autonomous house. But the ensuing and brief description in the appendix envisages a super-insulated structure with low ventilation rates to minimize heating demand, with a form dictated by the need for large south-facing areas for solar collection, and a conservatory to provide passive solar gains and to permit indoor food production.

The Vales had clearly served their apprenticeship on the Autarkic House and some similar approaches emerge in the Autonomous House, but with a low-key and appropriate or alternative technological theme. The north side of the house had

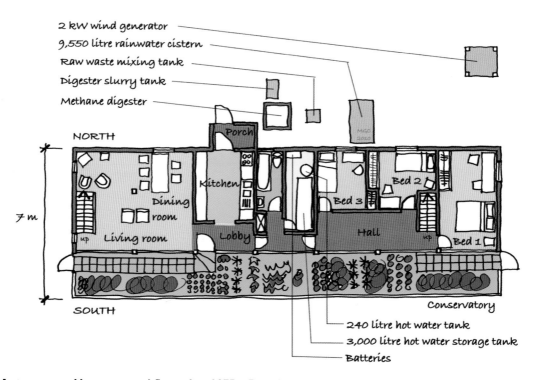

2 kW wind generator
9,550 litre rainwater cistern
Raw waste mixing tank
Digester slurry tank
Methane digester

NORTH

Porch

Kitchen

Dining room

Living room

up

Lobby

Bed 3

Bed 2

Hall

up

Bed 1

7 m

SOUTH

Conservatory

240 litre hot water tank
3,000 litre hot water storage tank
Batteries

Autonomous House: ground floor plan, 1975 – Brenda and Robert Vale.

Autonomous House: cross-section, 1975 – Brenda and Robert Vale.

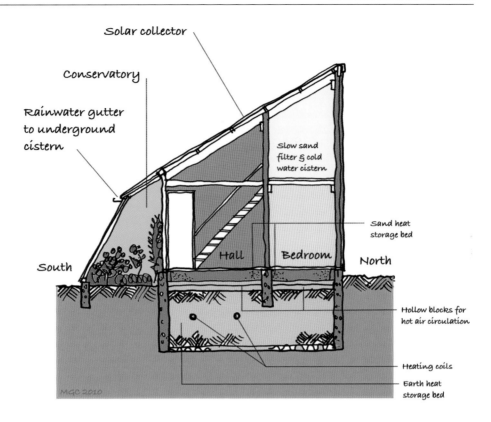

Solar collector

Conservatory

Rainwater gutter to underground cistern

Slow sand filter & cold water cistern

Sand heat storage bed

South

Hall

Bedroom

North

Hollow blocks for hot air circulation

Heating coils

Earth heat storage bed

MGC 2010

few windows to reduce heat losses and the attic storey was closed off in winter with insulating shutters to save heating energy. The large expanse of raking, south-facing roof houses solar collectors that heat hot water and act to top-up passive solar gains to heat the house. The basement contained a long-term thermal storage battery of earth, which was charged from the 2kW windmill after it has provided energy for lighting, refrigerator and other small electrical loads.

Rainwater was collected from the large roof and stored in an underground cistern, pumped up to a holding tank in the attic and sand-filtered through a gravity-fed system until pure enough for drinking – waste washing water was also purified and re-used. The Autonomous House also had a methane digester, whose heat was topped up by recovering heat from waste washing water. Livestock manure, human and vegetable waste were used in the digester to produce enough gas for cooking. The Vales claimed that the Autonomous House could

be built for the same price per square metre as a traditional brick-built house in the 1970s.

Tantalizingly, they ended with the notion that the Autonomous House was due to be built in Middlesex, where it would have been used as student accommodation for Brunel University on a site of nearly a hectare in area. But, the book certainly provided a counter-culture staple for architectural students of this era, to rival the Whole Earth Catalogue. Sadly, it was not until much later that the Vales built an autonomous house, by which time it was called The New Autonomous House – although they did refurbish a building and live autonomously in the 1970s and 1980s.

BLACK GOLD AND THE BRITISH HOUSE

Five Decades of Energy Efficiency?
In a temperate climate like the United Kingdom, around half the energy used in houses is to heat

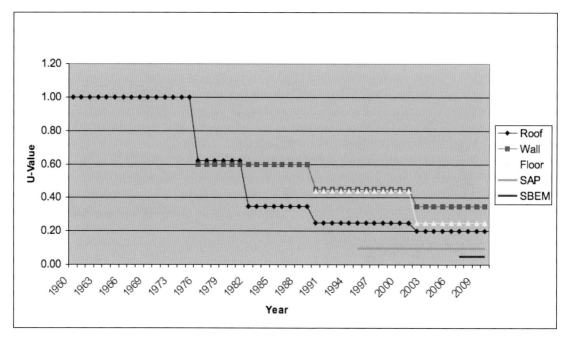

UK building regulations – slow evolution of building fabric U-values.

the dwellings in winter – particularly if the building envelope heat losses are large and rapid from un-insulated walls and roofs, and single-glazing. In the UK it has taken half-a-century for regulatory U-values, or rates of heat loss from domestic building fabric, to reach anywhere near the 'super-insulation' standards that were advocated and used in leading-edge designs in the 1960s and 1970s.

It appears that, if the old adage is 'stick, carrot and peer pressure', we will have to increase the latter two, rather than relying solely on regulation. In the 1960s, coal supplied three-quarters of all energy, and it was not until 1964 that the first modern building regulations were introduced that considered insulation – they introduced a requirement for an inch (25mm) thickness of roof insulation only (U-value of 1.0W/m^{2}K, heat rises – after all). Meanwhile, the revolutionary Wallasey School in Liverpool was built in the early 1960s, with 130mm of external insulation and no heating system.

Wallasey School had a large expanse of south-facing double-glazing, with movable insulation – for passive solar gain – with good thermal mass in the exposed concrete floors and masonry walls. Auxiliary heat was provided from the electric lights and occupants, but the airtightness did lead to some odours. It operated successfully for many years as a school, and was recently refurbished for use as a conserved, listed building. A third of the energy reductions came from the carefully thought-out, passive, solar-design strategy, which obviated the need for a heating system. The architect, Emslie A. Morgan, had auto-didactically imbibed sufficient scientific principles to propose such an original approach – sadly he died three years after the school was opened in 1961, before he could leave a further legacy.

1970s

This decade of oil-price shocks, coal miners' strikes and political turmoil brought the three-day working week to the UK for a while, for all the wrong reasons – energy shortages. The Middle Eastern conflict and restricted oil supplies saw the price of crude oil go from $3 to $12 a barrel. Such shortage of supply at least had the effect of pushing

Dr M. King Hubbert's (Geophysicist) predicted peak of world oil production slightly further out, than the fifty years from 1956. However, we must have reached it by now, in 2010 – if Professor Al Bartlett's 'essential exponential' message is anything to go by, particularly with a burgeoning population (nearly tripled since 1950). Twenty-five per cent inflation rates in mid1970s Britain did not help with fuel prices.

The UK Government ran the 'Better insulated house programme' from 1973 to 1984, conceived in response to the energy crisis; the programme monitored the effect of loft and cavity wall insulation to 180 homes. Modest savings were shown, but occupants also sought better comfort conditions, so that average internal temperatures rose from 13 to 19°C. The programme showed that work on heating controls, thermal mass, air leakage, heat transfer through party walls and super-insulation were needed – but the work did set the standards for the 1982 building regulations. Meanwhile the 1976 building regulations improved roof U-values to $0.6W/m^2K$ and introduced a U-value of $0.6W/m^2K$ for walls.

In 1976, *A House of the Future* was aired on Granada TV as a topical response to the 'energy crisis'. It ran for thirteen weekly episodes, focusing on one area of 'technology' each week. The House was an attempt to turn a brick barn in Macclesfield into an 'eco-house', with a volunteer family living in it – eco-reality TV long before *Big Brother*. Amongst the technologies were: high levels of insulation (e.g. 150mm in the roof); $42m^2$ of solar panels; a 3,400-ltr rock heat store; heat pumps; conservatory; wind turbine; energy-saving fittings; and mechanical ventilation with heat recovery from the kitchen. The series must have boosted sales of the Vales' autonomous house publication, which hit the bookshelves in the previous year – while the theoretical Autarkic House project continued amidst the courts, towers and spires of Cambridge.

The main lesson from a few months 'on location' in Macclesfield was that high thermal mass with good insulation led to good comfort conditions – which combined the three aspects of insulation, airtightness and heat recovery that really worked.

More tellingly, for all involved, was the conversion of the eco-house (a product) into the lessons for a green and sustainable lifestyle (a process). In the same year, an experimental house at the Centre for Alternative Technology in mid-Wales used 450mm of insulation in the walls, quadruple glazing and a heat pump – it remains the best-insulated house in Britain, and the extra costs were £1,000, giving a seven-year payback period. In the late 1970s, prototype 'solar houses' showed that energy demands could be halved.

1980s

Crude-oil prices reached $20 a barrel in 1979 and then rose steeply to just over $50 a barrel with the advent of the Iran–Iraq War and the Iranian Revolution, but came back down again to $20 a barrel by the end of the 1980s. The term 'monergy' was coined, while the 1982 building regulations set U-values of $0.6W/m^2K$ for walls and $0.35W/m^2K$ for roofs. The Pennyland and Linford House projects involved the extensive monitoring of 177 houses and detailed monitoring of eight homes, which were insulated well above current building regulation levels (in fact, better than the 1995 building regulations would be). Average total fuel-use was calculated at 169kWh/m²/year, with annual CO_2 levels of 6.1 tonnes/year (2.2 space heating; 1.7 hot water; 0.6 cooking; and 1.6 lighting and appliances). The Pennyland House had annual CO_2 levels of 4.3 tonnes/year (1.5 space heating; 1.0 hot water; 0.3 cooking; and 1.5 lighting and appliances). These houses showed that passive solar-design approaches worked, but had a marginal benefit with high levels of insulation – they were cost-effective, buildable and airtight (5.4 air changes/hour at 50Pa of pressure).

The Milton Keynes Energy Park opened with a flourish in the 1985 and included tours of a number of energy efficient show homes, such as Feilden Clegg Architect's 'Solar Courtyard House'. The house was super-insulated with super-glazing U-values of $0.9W/m^2K$; mechanical ventilation with heat recovery (MVHR); and a condensing boiler. Total fuel use was 170kWh/m²/year. The super-glazing was not much of an advance on smaller areas of double-glazing; MVHR needed airtight construction; and the early condensing boiler was unreliable. The Two Mile Ash houses at Milton Keynes, also built in 1985, were also super-insulated; airtight; contained thermal storage; and mechanical ventilation with heat recovery – their total fuel use was 165kWh/m^2/year. Although the thermal store was not working any better than the Macclesfield house a decade earlier, the MVHR worked, as did the airtight construction (1.6 air changes/hour at 50Pa pressure).

The barrier of 100kWh/m^2/year for total fuel usage was broken in the late-1980s with the Warmhome 200 in Newtownabbey, Northern Ireland. The house featured a permanent shuttering construction system to achieve U-values below 0.2W/m^{2}K. Other features were an electric boiler and MVHR, which contributed to the achievement of a total fuel consumption of 80kWh/m^2/year. The cost savings on the reduced heating system easily covered the cost of the extra insulation.

1990s

The 1990s saw the Kyoto Climate Change Convention (1997) to combat global warming and climate change, ratified by most industrialized nations of the world, with the exception of the United States of America. The price of a barrel of crude oil had reduced to $15 by 1999, but spiked briefly up to $25 with the advent of the First Gulf War. The 1990 building regulations saw U-values improve to: roof = 0.25, walls = 0.45, floors = 0.45W/m^{2}K. The 1995 building regulations retained the same U-values, but introduced a U-value of 3.3W/m^{2}K for windows for the first time, and saw the introduction of the Standard Assessment Procedure (SAP), which rated the energy efficiency of houses on a percentage scale.

The UK Government's Energy Efficiency Best Practice programme (EEBPp) launched a project to identify 'ultra-low-energy homes' – of seventy-four schemes identified, twelve were selected for detailed monitoring and four houses met the selection target of total energy use less than the magical 100kWh/m^2/year. Lower Watts House (1992) achieved a total fuel use of around 70kWh/m^2/year, with super-insulation (U-values of 0.2W/m^{2}K), attention to detailed design to avoid thermal bridging, and airtight construction (3.6 air changes/hour at 50Pa pressure). The Oxford Eco House (1994) claimed net zero carbon dioxide through the use of super-insulation (U-values of 0.2W/m^{2}K), a 4kW photo-voltaic panel array covering the entire south-facing roof, solar direct hot-water and gas-condensing boiler.

Three standards of zero-carbon house were proposed by the EEBPp: zero carbon dioxide; zero

The south elevation of the Oxford Eco House, 1994.

heating; and autonomous. Zero CO_2 means that renewable energy production must balance the use of fossil fuels, or green tariff electricity can be used. Zero heating means that space heating requirements are met by solar and other heat gains. And autonomous means that on-site renewables meet all annual energy needs – effectively an amalgamation of the previous two standards. The autonomous house could be energy grid-linked (allow for the export of renewable energy from the house to the grid) with on-site water supply and sewage disposal. As a comparison, the average 1930s house used 400kWh/m²/year (8 tonnes of CO_2/year); a typical house built to building regulations in the mid-1990s used 200kWh/m²/year (4 tonnes of CO_2/year); while the three standards were, respectively:

- Zero CO_2 = 100kWh/m²/year (2 tonnes of CO_2/year).
- Zero heating = 50kWh/m²/year (1 tonnes of CO_2/year).
- Autonomous = 25kWh/m²/year (0.5 tonnes of CO_2/year).

Clearly, these standards did not include behavioural aspects outside the house, such as using the family car for 12,500 miles a year at 35 mpg (4.5 tonnes CO_2); a long-haul flight for a family holiday (3 tonnes CO_2); or the family's food for a year (8 tonnes CO_2).

The latter years of the decade saw the Department of the Environment's Green House Programme, which targeted 100 public sector demonstration homes with insulation, heating, ventilation, lighting, CHP and tenant advice. The York Energy Demonstration Project targeted existing terraced homes and showed that half of the carbon dioxide reduction measures were cost-effective, condensing boilers work and that central heating was not necessary. Brenda and Robert Vale designed and built the New Autonomous House in Southwell, which included super-insulation, thermal mass, heat recovery ventilators, woodstove, rainwater collection and composting toilets. The Hockerton Housing Project proved that houses could be designed without a heating system, and

smashed the autonomous house standard with a total fuel use of just 10kWh/m²/year.

2000s

The beginning of the twenty-first century heralded the coining of the phrase 'sustainability' with the triple bottom-line of environmental, economic and social sustainability. The price of crude oil rapidly increased to around $50 a barrel with the start of the Second Gulf War. The 2002 building regulations improved U-values to: roof = 0.20, walls = 0.35, floors = 0.25, windows = 0.20W/m²K. It has taken at least three decades to legislate for levels of insulation approaching super-insulation, which has been advocated and shown as cost-effective since the 1970s.

Twenty-five energy-efficient homes built in Collingwood, Nottinghamshire, by Gusto Homes, show that super-insulation, solar hot water, condensing boilers, mechanical ventilation with heat recovery, rainwater collection and wood boilers can be achieved in the speculative housing market. The Nottingham Ecohome shows that it can also be done to an existing Victorian terraced house. The Beddington Zero Energy Development (2001) in South London was the first attempt to create a large zero-carbon community, using super-insulation, passive ventilation with heat recovery, biofuel CHP, photovoltaic solar collectors, water and waste management, and a sustainable travel strategy.

Lessons learnt?

- Every design-decision affects energy use.
- Energy efficiency is cost-effective.
- Energy efficiency first – energy supply second.
- Technology grants are often dangerous.
- Airtightness is generally poorly understood.
- Daylight is paramount and people like it.
- Auxillary energy loads can dominate.
- Conservatories are often a false economy – they end up being heated!

Finally, after fifty years of effort, fuel use and carbon dioxide emissions are still rising, as global population burgeons. An 80 per cent reduction in CO_2 levels by 2050 requires an enormous effort, but

The Nottingham Ecohome, 2003.

one that should be encouraged by the future uncertainty of energy supplies in the UK, not to mention increasing evidence of ecological disaster and local catastrophes. But vested interests still hold us back.

CHAPTER SUMMARY

• We have sought autonomy and self-sufficiency in our dwellings since ancient times. The Roman architect Vitruvius advocated orienting houses to the south to benefit from passive solar energy and advised that house plans should take advantage of the path of the sun throughout the day. Solar energy influenced urban planning and house design until the discovery of electricity a century or so ago.

• The evolution of attempts at zero-carbon houses, or at least autonomous or self-sufficient dwellings, stretches back many decades, at least until the middle of the twentieth century. The radical American architect Buckminster Fuller developed the Dymaxion House in the 1930s. He was trying to produce an efficient 'machine for living in', that was mass-produced, cost-effective and efficiently operated, with low environmental impacts; an autonomous and self-sufficient dwelling that was lightweight,

- portable, energy efficient, self-ventilating, self-temperature regulating and self-cleaning.
- Buckminster Fuller was born in 1895 and died at the age of 88. He was a polymath, practical philosopher and pioneer environmentalist. After some early failures he devoted all of his life to making the world work for the benefit of all humanity, mainly through his ideas and interventions in the built environment. The development of the geodesic dome and Dymaxion Globe are among his most notable achievements. The Buckminster Fuller Institute in New York is devoted to his legacy.
- The Dymaxion 'Wichita' House of 1947 was Buckminster Fuller's prototype autonomous house that was intended for mass production to provide a low-cost, low-environmental impact, energy-efficient solution to post-war mass-housing problems. They were circular in plan with a central services' core with a 'dome effect' natural ventilation system, facilitated by a rotating wind catcher on the roof.
- The Cambridge Autarkic House was developed throughout the 1970s by a team of architects and engineers at the Cambridge School of Architecture. It was underpinned by painstaking research into the practical achievement of energy and resource autonomy for the nuclear family in a rural location. The main objective of the project was to create a prototype house that was independent of mains' utilities, so that it could be positioned anywhere in the world. It was intended to have low energy demand satisfied by passive and active means.
- One of the key concepts of the Autarkic House was that during the winter months, of inclement weather at least, the occupants would retreat into the fully insulated half of the house to conserve heat and energy. During the summer, and probably for most of the year, the double-height conservatory would accumulate solar gains and provide a spacious amenity and large greenhouse for crop cultivation.
- The Autarkic House was conceived as a completely self-sufficient dwelling with a compact shape (roughly a cube), with a super-insulated fabric, with large areas of glazing in the conservatory allowing passive solar gain and food cultivation. Construction was timber-framed with a central steel tower to support the wind turbine, with thermal mass provided from reinforced-concrete floors and partitions.
- The energy demand of the Autarkic House was reduced by using approaches such as heavy insulation, heat recovery, reducing air infiltration, water-saving spray taps and showers, fluorescent lighting tubes and a cold-water washing-machine. This reduced energy use to less than a third of a contemporary detached house. Renewable energy from solar panels and a wind turbine were used to satisfy this much reduced energy demand. Drinking water was purified from rainwater collected from the roof, and an experimental sewage digester obviated the need for mains connection.
- The Autonomous House was the subject and title of a book published by Brenda and Robert Vale in 1975 – defined as a 'house operating independently of any inputs except those of its immediate environment'. They provided several chapters of information and 'data' covering performance specification aspects of the autonomous house, and some brief architectural proposals in a appendix – summarized as an appropriate technological response to the problem, which could be built for the same price as a contemporaneous brick-built house of the same floor area.
- Since the energy crisis of the 1970s, legislative progress for energy efficiency in the UK has been slow, despite a number of successful government initiatives and successful case study houses, which have shown the cost-effectiveness of increased insulation levels, building fabric airtightness and heat recovery. Other symbolic features, such as conservatories, have proved a false economy if they are heated. Fuel use and carbon dioxide emissions are still rising with global population growth, so that future targets for sustainability are challenging – but increasing evidence for ecological disaster should provide incentives for collective action and cooperation, despite the adverse efforts of vested interests.

CHAPTER 3

Old Houses

There is no question of expediency or feeling whether we shall preserve the buildings of past times or not. We have no right whatever to touch them. They are not ours. They belong partly to those who built them, and partly to all the generations of mankind who are to follow us.

William Morris (1877)

ANCIENT HISTORY

The Greeks and Romans were well aware of the power of the sun to heat their homes, or passive solar architecture as we call it these days. In their native lands, the climate dictated that domestic architecture should largely exclude the powerful sun to create shady courtyards or atriums. The use of stone, brick and clay roof-tiles also ensured that their houses contained enough heavyweight building materials to absorb the sun's heat during the day and release it again during the colder nights. This heavy thermal mass evened out the temperature to more comfortable levels. The Roman architect Vitruvius, recommended that houses should face south, in the northern hemisphere, to benefit from the warmth of the sun in the middle of winter. He also thought that bedrooms and kitchens should face east so that they were warmed, both physically and psychologically, from the rising sun in the morning.

As the Roman Empire expanded north, heating houses became more important. Archaeological evidence shows that most of the Roman villas scattered around the northern countryside had under-floor heating, or hypocausts. This ancient central heating must have consumed vast amounts of energy from the timber in the forests, not to men-

tion its labour-intensiveness; but that was of little concern to the Romans in a slave-based economy and largely surrounded by trees. However, the Romans can possibly lay claim to the first energy-efficient buildings at Bath in England, where they used geothermal heating. After the fall of the Roman Empire, domestic architecture returned to more primitive wooden-framed architecture, much more thermally-lightweight, apart from some clay in wattle-and-daub construction. The energy preoccupation for the majority of the population during these centuries was the provision of heat for cooking and space heating.

Timber-framed buildings were made reasonably comfortable, and with enough straw the thatched roof might even match the thermal properties of a modern roof. Even the infill of the timber framing, made of wattle, mud, straw and animal hair, might be built up enough to provide modest levels of thermal insulation. In many ways such a house might be more comfortable than a stone house, where tapestries were placed on the walls to take some of the chill away from cold stone walls. At least in the timber house the organic nature of the construction meant that it could be improved, and repaired, quite easily from materials to hand, and draught-stripping could be affected with animal hair or vegetable fibres.

MEDIEVAL HOUSES

Most, if not all houses built before 1700 benefit from heritage protection laws throughout the world, as they are invariably comparatively rare survivals. They are sustainable because they are still with us after several centuries, in many cases. The embodied energy that went in to their construction, both materials and labour, must have been repaid many decades or even centuries ago; but their running, and particularly heating, costs rarely create zero carbon dioxide emissions. Fortunately, there are many ways in which even a protected medieval house can approach the zero-carbon ideal – the reduction of carbon dioxide emissions due to heating and heat loss is the obvious place to start in colder climates. In warmer climates, such as the Mediterranean, old houses are invariably thermally heavyweight to keep them cool in summer. This should obviate the need for energy and carbon-expensive modern interventions such as air conditioning and mechanical ventilation.

Opportunities for improving energy and environmental performance are largely restricted to increasing loft insulation, carefully improving air leakage and improved technology, such as lighting, heating and controls. Many medieval houses, particularly more modest survivals with limited protection, will have sustained damage due to inappropriate or inadequate repairs and maintenance at some stage in their history. Inept attempts to improve medieval buildings, in terms of their energy efficiency or otherwise, show the importance of proper research and professional advice when undertaking work to ancient houses. Clearly, the first place to start any attempt to approach carbon zero is through energy efficiency, such as:

• Good management – maintaining equipment properly; setting controls correctly; switching equipment off when not in use; adopting appropriate modern technologies; and carefully considered draughtproofing to avoid excessive air infiltration.

Energy efficient medieval cottage in Hertfordshire, 1687.

- Controls improvements – particularly temperature and time controls, and adding heating-zone controls to avoid overheating unoccupied rooms. One of the most effective ways to save energy is to turn the heating down – for which it helps to have a means of control to start with! Typically, a room thermostat might be set to around 21°C. If this is reduced to 20°C, heating energy consumption can be reduced by 6–10 per cent. Wearing warmer clothing and reducing the temperature to 19°C or even 18°C will have corresponding savings. However, most medieval building fabric and fittings will need minimal temperature levels to conserve them. The National Trust does not allow the temperature of its properties to fall below 5°C when they are empty and closed up for the winter, and pursues a strategy of 'conservation heating'. This is a way of avoiding extremes of internal humidity by the control of temperature.

- Conservation heating – the National Trust has used the idea of 'conservation heating' since the 1980s to ensure a balance between temperature and humidity in its properties – this seldom raises the temperature by more than 5°C above the outside temperature, which generally maintains a relative humidity (RH) of about 50–65 per cent – a good compromise for most materials – this is why radiators may sometimes be on in the summer if the weather is humid. (Conversely, on a chilly, dry day in winter, after the NT's houses have been closed for the season, some visitors would find the places far too cold for comfort.) The amount of energy required is typically around a third of that required for 'comfort heating'. However, most NT properties are closed up for the winter, with minimal heating levels, but some compromise between conservation and comfort heating may suit occupants of ancient houses.

- Insulation improvements – carefully considered increases in insulation levels, particularly in the roof. Insulation improvements to the floor and walls are usually more difficult and may reduce the ability of the house to 'breathe'. Natural insulation materials, such as sheep's wool, are particularly sympathetic to medieval houses, as it is hygroscopic, which means that it allows moisture to pass through it, helping the house to 'breathe'. Like most traditional building materials, sheep's wool absorbs moisture during wet periods and then evaporates it in dry spells – working in harmony with the ancient building fabric. However, the introduction of impervious modern insulation may be detrimental, unless very carefully considered and detailed.

- Windows and doors improvements – carefully considered draughtstripping to reduce infiltration, but not to totally exclude natural ventilation, is usually the best course. Obviously, original components should be retained and conserved. Replacement double-glazing is usually completely inappropriate and will invariably destroy the original character of windows and doors. Secondary glazing is usually a good option, and SPAB advises that this should be removable, unobtrusive and use non-reflective glass.

- Heating system improvements – to improve efficiency and reduce fuel cost and consumption. Improvements to insulation levels and optimizing natural ventilation levels should result in a reduced heating boiler size. Technologies such as condensing boilers are worth considering. There are a number of

Solar thermal panels on a rural cottage.

Villa Rotunda near Venice, designed by Andrea Palladio in 1567.

myths surrounding condensing boilers, which are largely allayed in guidance from the Energy Saving Trust (EST). Their publication is downloadable from their website: 'CE 52 (GIL 74) Domestic condensing boilers – the benefits and the myths'.

- Hot water – solar thermal panels are a good way to pre-heat hot water and are easily retrofitted to older houses.
- Lighting improvements – low-energy lightbulbs are an easy and non-intrusive energy efficiency improvement to install in medieval houses.

EIGHTEENTH-CENTURY HOUSES

The late-medieval period ushered in a classical revival in domestic architecture in both Europe and the New World. The Renaissance recast the ancient classical architectural rules with a stress on harmonious proportions and symmetry. Local vernacular traditions throughout the world were 'gentrified' into symmetrical facades, usually with a central and architecturally celebrated front door flanked by a symmetrical displacement of windows. Legislation, to avoid the fires that often ravaged groups of close-knit timber medieval buildings, made brickwork a ubiquitous building material, while architectural pattern-books ensured a harmony of detail.

Fortunately, the classical proportioning systems ensured high-ceiling heights for good, natural ventilation and daylight penetration. Many rural dwellings of this time were also oriented to take advantage of passive solar gains during winter. However, householders had much lower expectations of comfort in this era, and whole-house heating was unheard of – heating was still very much a luxury. This ensured that eighteenth-century houses were far nearer to carbon-zero ideals than many modern houses, apart from the use of solid fuels, such as coal.

Heating

Heating has evolved from a luxury into something of a commonplace extravagance for many people. Historically, people wore more layers of heavy clothing, wore their hats indoors, and furniture included such features as upholstered wings to take the chill off the many draughts in houses. Even as recently as 1970, the average UK house was heated to a temperature of only 12°C; this had risen to 18°C by 2003, and has probably risen by another degree or two now. Some lifestyle compromises are usually necessary to live in a Georgian house, but they can often be for the better and embrace the original spirit of the Georgian age, in a modern zero-carbon manner.

The architectural history television presenter Dan Cruickshank, has gone as far as trying to live an authentic Georgian lifestyle in his house in the Spitalfields area of London. He admits that the house is cold, but he wears a hat indoors and his Georgian furniture is designed to take some of the chill off – such as upholstered 'wings' to help insulate him from draughts. Candlelight can also lend the ambience of contrasting light that we often lack in our modern lifestyles!

Lighting

Well-designed artificial lighting schemes, focusing on task and accent lighting rather than high levels of ambient light are desirable in high-ceiling and well day-lit Georgian houses. Inefficient tungsten, incandescent lightbulbs are quickly being phased out of production – 90 per cent of the energy they use is given off as heat rather than light. Energy-efficient lightbulbs only consume about 20 per cent of the energy of incandescent, tungsten lightbulbs. LED lighting, or light emitting diodes, are clearly the future of low-carbon lighting, as they can last for decades and emit a very small amount of heat. Finally, make sure that you switch lights off that you are not using, and keep bulbs and fixtures clean – in pursuit of the zero-carbon Georgian house.

Light emitting diode (LED) bulbs.

Windows

The invention of the double-hung sash window in the late-seventeenth century was a high-point of British architectural development. The double-hung sash window opens at the top and bottom to aid good ventilation. Draughtstripping and secondary glazing are the only real options to improve the thermal efficiency of Georgian windows – while a 20mm air-gap is optimal for thermal insulation, a gap of 150mm is preferable for sound insulation. As many Georgian houses are in urban terraces, somewhere between the two should give a suitable compromise. Georgian window shutters are a useful way to improve window insulation when they are closed at night and they can even have their thermal efficiency increased with added insulation.

Nineteenth-Century Houses

The industrial revolution and new world trade and technology ushered in the ubiquitous suburban house in most parts of the world. The new battle for the domestic, suburban housing market was a fierce one between speculative builders and the rapidly increasing ranks of professional architects – by the 1870s, architects were using the new religion of sanitation as a major weapon in their armoury. The promotion of the 'artistic house' garnered the middle to higher end of the suburban market for

Victorian villas in
North London.

architects, and builders sought to superficially emulate the aesthetics and styles of these vanguard dwellings in cheaper, mass-housing schemes. Ultimately, the trinity of sanitation, planning and artistic aesthetics was adapted to lesser budgets and pervaded burgeoning middle-class suburbia.

Terraced housing of this period is inherently a model of sustainable development in terms of compactness, interconnection, mixed-use and affordability. Recent studies of sustainable-housing forms recommend close study of such housing estates and adaptation of their layout principles to contemporary development. The architectural form of the terraced housing from this era is still regularly reinterpreted in modern housing developments. Traditional domestic construction tech-

Manchester Victorian Terraces SAVE'd

The Pathfinder Initiative was a controversial attempt to demolish Victorian terraced houses in inner-city areas, rather than refurbishing them. SAVE Britain's Heritage was active in collaborating with residents in areas such as East Manchester, to find alternative ways to preserve and retrofit several hundred Victorian terraced houses. Toxteth Street is the centre of an area of humble but attractive Victorian terraced housing, where over 400 houses were scheduled for compulsory purchase and destruction, to make way for a new housing development. The coalition of residents and SAVE fought the initiative, arguing that the houses were well built and should be refurbished to retain local character and densities.

Mark Hines Architects was commissioned to demonstrate how the old houses could be sustainably refurbished to offer a range of accommodation and outdoor spaces. Their plans to join, extend and modify the existing properties showed the flexibility of the Victorian terraced-house typology, and created homes of up to four bedrooms with gardens to the rear. The re-think retained the embodied energy of the existing houses and increased their energy efficiency and sustainability. William Palin, Secretary of SAVE, said that the scheme 'exposed the insanity of the demolition plans. Judged on community benefits, environmental impact and cost, rehabilitation and refurbishment are clearly the way forward. It is less destructive, helps preserve the existing community, saves money and offers revitalisation without losing the enduring qualities of these characterful and much-loved terraced streets'.

niques did not change much over this period. It was only in the more avant garde houses that cavity walls were first experimented with, until their more widespread use after 1920. Rainwater-collection systems were common in rural houses in the northern hemisphere, and obviously ubiquitous in the more arid regions of the southern hemisphere, a feature that we are only beginning to re-invent now in sustainable and zero-carbon houses.

Energy Conservation

Refurbishment of solid-walled houses can achieve energy efficiencies equal to, or better than, those of new-build properties. The energy efficient measures generally most cost-effective in solid-walled houses are:

- Loft insulation.
- Insulated dry lining to external walls – or external insulating render.
- Ground-floor insulation.
- Secondary glazing.
- Gas central heating with condensing boiler.
- Factory-insulated hot-water cylinder.
- Controlled ventilation system.

Roof Spaces

Around two-thirds of domestic energy use is usually used for space heating. Heat rises, and the roof is

Loft insulation installed in the roof space of a post-war bungalow.

the part of the house most exposed to the weather, so it follows that insulating the loft is a good starting point to improve the performance of an existing house. Insulating the loft space is a relatively easy option, where ventilation to the roof space must be maintained, usually with eaves' ventilators. Other issues include the need for a boarded access path to get to the water tank, where the insulation covers ceiling joists; and the insulation of water tanks to prevent them freezing in a colder attic. Using a natural insulation material, such as sheep's wool, means that slightly less thickness is needed, and it is easier to work with than mineral wool/fibre materials. Recycled glass insulation is also good. Rooms in the roof are technically trickier.

Room in the Roof

Insulation improvements at rafter level to a pitched roof are more complicated than improving insulation at ceiling level. Although such upgrades are practical at any time, they are most cost-effective when the loft is being converted into a habitable space, or when the roof covering is being replaced. If the roof covering has reached the end of its life and it is time to replace it with new tiles, this also presents the opportunity to insulate the roof at rafter level to create what is know technically as a 'warm roof'.

A warm roof is created when rigid insulation is placed above the roof structure The term 'warm roof' refers to the fact that the structure is on the warm side of the insulation. Opting for a warm-roof insulation improvement means that there is no need for ventilation or a vapour control barrier, as there is no 'thermal bridge' to create a cold surface for condensation. Alternatively, adding insulation to create a 'cold-roof' upgrade requires roof ventilation, from one eaves to the other, and also at the ridge for roof pitches over 35 degrees. A vapour-control layer is also required, usually behind the raking plasterboard lining of the room-in-the-roof ceiling. Headroom in the attic room is sometimes an issue with this type of insulation upgrade, but there are insulation products as thin as 20–25mm, which have good U-values, if headroom is at a premium. If it is not so crucial, it may be possible to place insulation in between the

ABOVE: **Recycled glass insulation – three bottles provides a 2.5m² roll.**

rafters, as well as underneath them, so that the rafter no longer acts as a thermal bridge. But when placing insulation between rafters, a ventilation space of at least 50mm should be left above the insulation.

Interstitial condensation, which is condensation between or within the layers of the roof construction, is risked if inadequate ventilation is provided, or if the vapour-control layer is placed in the wrong position. Interstitial condensation may still occur in the cold-roof upgrade to a traditional building, as the roof structure still needs to breathe – and the introduction of an impervious, vapour-control layer (e.g. a polythene sheet) is more appropriate for modern houses. For a traditional house, it is more appropriate to use a vapour check of much lower vapour resistance than a polythene membrane, such as a modern 'breather' membrane.

TWENTIETH-CENTURY HOUSES

The end of the First World War provided the catalyst for mass social housing in Europe and across

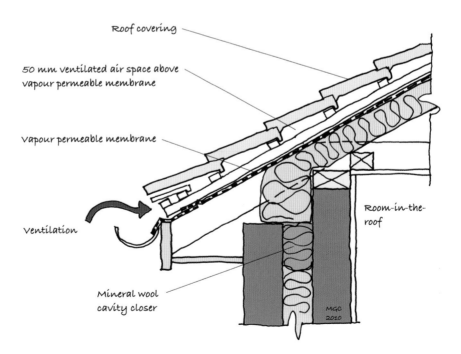

Roof covering

50 mm ventilated air space above vapour permeable membrane

Vapour permeable membrane

Ventilation

Room-in-the-roof

Mineral wool cavity closer

MGC 2010

Room-in-the-roof with vapour barrier and ventilation roof.

the world. Returning combatants were offered a new deal, which included 'homes fit for heroes'. Over four million dwellings were built in council estates during the inter-war years in Britain. Many of these were constructed using non-traditional building techniques, due to shortages of labour and materials. Inter-war private housing developments were usually of a lower density, causing problems of 'ribbon' and 'pepper-pot' development, made possible by low petrol prices. Ribbon developments, only one house deep and along arterial roads, exacerbated the perception of housing incursion into rural areas, among other problems. Pepper-pot developments, on the other hand, made vehicular access more difficult, as they were isolated houses in rural locations.

Sprawling housing development led to legislation that heralded modern planning laws in most countries, but most towns and cities were still planned around the automobile in the Western world. Even as late as the 1970s, the British new town of Milton Keynes was laid out around vehicular access, using town-planning precedents such as those of Los Angeles. The political oil shocks of the mid-1970s provided a much needed spur to energy efficiency and alternative sources of energy, as an economic and national necessity. But it also increased the West's dependence on coal and nuclear power. The former, obviously, a major source of carbon dioxide emissions, and the latter lauded by some as an immediate way of reducing carbon dioxide emissions to ameliorate global warming and climate change.

The decades following the Second World War saw the philosophy of house construction changing towards that of industrialized building, with as much work as possible transferred from the site to the factory. However, public confidence waned after the Ronan Point collapse in 1968, which involved large panel, off-site construction. High-rise housing buildings were already controversial for social reasons, but Ronan Point raised technical doubts as well. Ronan Point was a twenty-two storey point-block with an inherently strong structure, but it was not designed to withstand the large gas explosion that caused its partial collapse. The explosion occurred in a corner flat on the eighteenth floor and caused the floors above to lift and the panels were blown outwards, leading to progressive collapse. Other construction problems were found in some of the other large-panel buildings. Volumetric systems, using a series of prefabricated 'boxes' that were connected on-site, were also used during the 1960s and 1970s. For ease of transportation, these usually involved lightweight timber or metal frames – following on from earlier volumetric aluminium bungalows from the immediate post-war period.

Cavity Walls

Cavity walls were occasionally used in buildings since at least the early decades of the nineteenth century, using a narrow cavity with brick or stone ties to hold the leaves of the construction together. They were usually used in prestigious buildings to improve comfort by reducing the passage of moisture to the interior of the building. The cavity wall became increasingly popular for widespread use in domestic architecture in the 1920s and 1930s, but still primarily as a 'rainscreen' to increase comfort and protect the inner leaf of the wall from being soaked by rainwater. The fact that it also promoted improved thermal comfort, with wider cavities, was, initially, an added benefit, and it was not until much later that insulation was added to the cavities in cavity-walled construction. The widespread use of insulation in cavity walls began in the 1970s and became part of the building regulations in the 1990s.

A solid wall of brickwork contains both 'header' and 'stretcher' bricks, with the header bricks acting to tie the construction together in brick bonds, such as English or Flemish bond. Cavity walls contain only stretcher bricks, or bricks placed lengthways, with a similar inner leaf, and both tied together with metal wall-ties that span the cavity. So it is easy to tell whether a wall is solid or in the then new-fangled cavity construction technique, simply by observing which type of brick bonding you have on your inter-wars house – even if the walls are rendered, there will usually be a plinth of brickwork, or some brickwork somewhere, as a tell-tale. Adding insulation to the wall cavity reduces heat loss through walls by up to 40 per cent, and is the most cost-effective single insulation measure after loft insulation.

Floors

Most eighteenth- and nineteenth-century houses, in towns and cities at least, were provided with a basement or cellar storey, but such hard-won and uneconomic space was unfashionable in the inter-wars speculative building boom. However, most inter-war houses were built with suspended timber floors, or a combination of solid and timber floors. Solid concrete floors followed a similar evolution to the cavity wall – beginning with an uninsulated solid floor laid on a DPM over hardcore, which conducts heat from the house directly into the ground. Heat is lost through a suspended timber floor via the gaps in the construction and the intentional draughts created by the air bricks that ventilate underneath the floor. The floor timbers would quickly become damp without such ventila-

tion and eventually rot away, but construction gaps in the floor should be improved to reduce draughts inside the house. Floorboards in suspended timber floors were later built with tongue-in-groove joints to reduce such draughts. It is only relatively recently that building regulations have required the addition of insulation to both types of ground floor, to meet improved U-value standards.

Solid, concrete floors were becoming popular in some of the leading housing developments in the late-nineteenth century, but most inter-war floors are usually constructed with at least some suspended timber joists and floorboards. Adding insulation to suspended timber floors is easiest if there is access from below, such as from a cellar or crawl space, or if the floor boards are being removed and replaced. This is also a good time to ensure that any water pipes below the floor are well-insulated. Adding insulation to a suspended timber floor should also improve airtightness and reduce draughts, but care should be taken to ensure the continuity of the insulation and necessary ventilation. A flexible sealant should be placed underneath the skirting board when it is replaced to reduce air gaps, but suspended timber floors need ventilation from airbricks, so these should not be blocked up.

TOP LEFT: **English bond brickwork.**

BOTTOM LEFT: **Flemish bond brickwork.**

BOTTOM RIGHT: **Stretcher bond brickwork.**

Refurbishing or replacing solid, concrete, ground floors or their screeds, also provides an ideal opportunity to add insulation. Solid, concrete slabs are the most difficult type of floor to retrofit with insulation. Adding rigid insulation on top of an existing solid floor will obviously raise the level of the new floor finish, so doors will need to be shortened. Some modern insulation materials are still effective, to a lesser extent, in very thin layers, so that increases to the floor levels are minimized. As a general rule, 25mm of polystyrene or 40mm of polyisocyanurate foam will improve the U-value of a solid floor to levels approaching modern building regulation standards. But a little added insulation is better than no insulation at all, and even only 5mm of rubber foam is better than nothing and will reduce heat loss through the floor and improve comfort levels.

Flat Roofs

The influence of the Modern Movement and architectural inspiration from continental Europe forged the International Style of architecture, which led to the use of flat roofs in domestic architecture of this era. Although flat-roofed houses were ultimately less popular than pitched-roof varieties, there are also many houses of this period that have acquired later flat-roofed extensions. Some of the original flat roofs were solid, reinforced concrete, the preferred construction material of Modern Movement architects. But the majority are likely to be constructed from timber, and if any insulation was subsequently added, it is invariably to the inside of the structural timber. This is known as a 'cold roof', because the structure is on the cold side of the insulation, i.e. nearer to the outside. The ventilation of cold roofs is essential, as the cold surface of the structure could cause condensation or interstitial condensation. It is possible to upgrade an uninsulated, timber, flat-roof by placing insulation between the joists that support the deck and waterproof membrane, but such 'cold roofs' are no longer recommended due to the difficulty of ensuring effective ventilation of the void – a 'warm roof' is preferred.

A warm-deck flat roof has insulation above the deck and joists, covered by a waterproof mem-brane – the structure elements are on the warm side of the construction, closest to the heated interior. A variation of the warm roof is called an 'inverted warm roof' – this is where rigid insulation is placed above the waterproof membrane and weighted down by stone chippings or paving slabs. If the waterproof membrane of the flat roof has reached the end of its life and is being replaced, a warm-roof upgrade should be considered. This also provides an opportunity to improve the drainage of a flat roof, by introducing tapered insulation, which should reduce the 'ponding' of rainwater. Rainwater that collects and lies in ponds on flat roofs due to inadequate falls to drainage outlets is a common problem – it increases the structural loading and reduces the life of the waterproof membrane, quite apart from looking unsightly and providing a potential breeding ground for aquatic insect life.

An inverted warm-roof solution is generally less preferable than a warm roof where the increased thickness of the subsequent roof construction is not problematic. And as the inverted warm-roof entails the addition of ballast material, the roof structure should be checked to ensure that it can take the additional weight, which this is rarely the case with timber flat-roof structures. It is also possible to create warm-roof constructions by applying a new waterproof membrane over the top of the existing waterproof membrane of an uninsulated roof. If it is not practical to increase the thickness of the roof with a warm-roof approach, internal insulation should be applied to the ceiling. Insulation-backed plasterboard is applied in a similar way to internal wall insulation, but to the ceiling, which has less risk of condensation than a cold-roof construction.

Similar principles, in terms of warm, cold and inverted roofs, apply to solid, concrete, flat-roofs. The generally preferred way of insulating a solid flat-roof is to add rigid insulation above the roof deck, making it a warm roof if the insulation is below the weatherproof membrane. The roof becomes an inverted warm-roof if the insulation is placed above the weatherproofing membrane, in which case a layer of ballast is placed on top to hold the insulation in place. Cleary, the retrofitted roof must be capable of withstanding the additional weight placed on it, particularly if a ballast layer is added, which could be quite heavy in the case of materials such as concrete paving slabs. This also provides opportunities, where the structure allows, to create roof terraces on top of retrofitted, solid flat-roofs.

Thermal Bridges

Most inter-war houses were constructed with little thought of thermal or cold bridges, as they were usually solid walled or uninsulated cavity walls. There was usually no consideration of the position of insulation in the construction layers, because there was usually no insulation when they were originally constructed! Heat will follow the easiest path from the heated interior space to the cold outdoors, the path with the least resistance. Solid elements, such as window sills or lintels over windows made of materials such as concrete or stone, which connect the warm inside and the cold exterior, make ideal cold or thermal bridges in the house's construction envelope. Clearly, such thermal bridges will significantly increase heat losses and heating costs in an old house, and because they

have a lower surface temperature than surrounding construction they will increase risks of internal condensation, damp and discomfort.

The only way to virtually eliminate thermal bridges when adding insulation to old houses is to adopt a 'warm overcoat' principle – to wrap the house in a continuous and contiguous layer of insulation. This would necessitate the use of external insulation to the walls and floors, as well as a warm-roof insulation upgrade. Such radical interventions are not always convenient, and are obviously only contemplated when a major refurbishment is underway, such as replacing old floors and roof coverings. They may also not be technically possible or aesthetically desirable. However, there are ways to minimize thermal bridging when adding layers of insulation internally, by considering the typical construction details of the house and ensuring careful attention to detail. After all, it would be a shame to partially undo all the good work done by insulating the house, by allowing thermal bridges to occur – and there is always the risk that you might introduce new problems, such as condensation, by not minimizing thermal bridges.

Re-roofing an inter-war house.

CASE STUDIES

Case Study: Camden Eco House, London

Key Points

- 1850s semi-detached solid-walled house in a conservation area.
- Target to achieve 80–90 per cent carbon dioxide reduction – virtual zero carbon.
- Monitoring of the property in use by University College London.
- Super-insulation to roof, external walls and floor.
- Double-glazed, high-performance replica sash windows.
- Air-leakage reduction and localized mechanical ventilation with heat recovery.
- Energy-efficient lighting throughout the property.

- 90 per cent efficient gas condensing boiler.
- Solar thermal and photovoltaic panels added to the roof.
- 11 tonnes of carbon dioxide per year saved.

General

17 Augustine Road is a typical property in North London, Victorian suburbia, which is now multi-tenancy and in the possession of Camden Council, who have refurbished it as a zero-carbon house exemplar project. Built in 1850, the house was given a new lease of low-energy life that reduced its carbon footprint by at least 80 per cent. The building fabric was upgraded by adding internal insulation to the solid, brick walls (95mm rigid insulation), increasing airtightness, and double-glazed replacement sash windows, which conserves its external character. The

Camden Eco House – next-door neighbour control house.

62

scheme went beyond English Heritage's recommendations in a conservation area, which proposed only 50–60 per cent reduction of the carbon footprint of the house, controversially removing some internal decoration, such as cornices, to achieve carbon zero, economically.

The scheme is intended as a pathfinder project, so conventional local authority contracts, materials and specifications were used – consequently, the scheme has the potential for wide replication across the borough. Economy also dictated the replacement of existing windows with new replicas that were about 25 per cent more energy efficient than introducing secondary glazing behind the original windows. The largest carbon-emission savings are reaped from the insulation improvements to the house's fabric, which, together with airtightness improvements and localized mechanical ventilation with heat recovery (MVHR), mean that flow rates of heated air escaping from the house are reduced by 80 per cent. A 90 per cent efficient condensing boiler was also added for hot-water supply.

Other features include high-performance solar thermal heating and an array of photovoltaic panels on the roof. The latter were a costly feature, at £20–30k, which was donated for research purposes – wider replication might follow when PVs become more economical. Sadly, the idea of a 3,000ltr rainwater-harvesting cistern was reluctantly rejected for reasons of capital cost, as was triple-glazing. Site area prevented the installation of a ground-source heat pump, and the over-cladding of the side and rear walls was rejected by the local planning council due to the restrictions of the conservation area.

The house is being monitored for two years by a team of experts from University College London, who will analyse energy consumption, temperature, humidity in the solid walls, air pressure and co-heating tests. They are using the unrefurbished, neighbouring house as a control benchmark. The results should provide the council with feedback for them to press-on with further zero carbon interventions to their existing housing stock, throughout the borough – not to mention give other local authorities the inspiration and confidence to do the same.

LEFT: **Camden Eco House – double-glazed replacement window detail.**

RIGHT: **Camden Eco House – entrance elevation.**

Case Study: Hyde Housing Association House, London

Hyde House – entrance elevation.

Key Points

- Late-1930s terraced house with cavity walls and suspended timber floors.
- Target to achieve 80 per cent carbon dioxide reduction – virtual zero carbon.
- Monitoring of the property in use for two years.
- Original SAP assessment of 60 (well above the UK average of 48).
- Airtightness testing revealed that the original construction was better than current building regulations.
- Super-insulation to roof, walls and floor.
- Double-glazing replaced with high-performance triple-glazing.

General

225 Court Farm Road in Mottingham, South London was constructed in the late-1930s as part of a large estate development. The brick cavity wall and suspended timber floor dwelling originally did not include an inside WC or bathroom, but later improvements included the addition of a first-floor shower room, the replacement of open fires with gas-fired central heating, and a rear extension containing a third bedroom with en suite bathroom. Previous building fabric improvements included poor quality double-glazing and 100mm loft insulation to the pitched roof – the flat-roofed extension only contained 25mm-thick mineral wool insulation. The suspended timber floor in the kitchen was also replaced with a solid, concrete one. The original water-supply plumbing was made from lead piping with an asbestos tank!

Mark Elton, a leading member of the RIBA Sustainable Futures Committee, and project architect with Energy Conscious Design (ECD) was appointed in early 2008. His initial proposals mooted the idea of a loft conversion, but this was ruled out due to a lack of headroom in the roof space. ECD commission SAP tests and discovered that the existing property scored a rating of 60 per cent (above the national average of 48 per cent) – the challenge was to achieve 80 per cent

Hyde House – PV array on flat roof of extension.

reductions in carbon emissions. Airtightness tests revealed surprising results and indicated that the house was better than current building regulations, but the windows were very leaky, followed by other openings, such as the loft hatch. Energy use for the existing premises was estimated at 209kWh/m^2/year, with CO_2 emissions of 70kg/m^2 (several tonnes in total).

Refurbishment

The overall strategy was to implement the simplest improvements and to do them very well to meet the virtual zero-carbon targets. The priorities were: to minimize heat losses from the building fabric; to install an easy copied, efficient form of space and water heating; to reduce the energy requirements for lighting; and to add the most appropriate forms of micro-generation renewable energy to reduce CO_2 emissions from the property. Super-insulation and replacement windows and doors addressed heat loss, combined with appropriate airtightness and MVHR. Phenolic foam rigid insulation was favoured for

Case Study: Hyde Housing Association House, London *(continued)*

Hyde House – rear garden elevation.

thermal performance and ease of installation, and impact on internal room dimensions (95mm thick). The rear extension was overclad with external panels with a silicone finish, and the roof with 220mm rigid polyurethane boards. U-value targets were:

- Suspended timber floor – 0.2W/m²K.
- External walls – 1.5W/m²K.
- Pitched or flat roofs – 0.1W/m²K.

The existing double-glazed windows were the weakest of building element in the airtightness test, so they were replaced with triple-glazed units with an overall U-value of 0.7W/m²K. The external doors were also replaced with new insulated doors with a U-value of 1.0W/m²K. Site workmanship and understanding of the ambitious targets were essential to success, so ECD held workshops with the construction team and issued large-scale drawings (1:5 scale) of abutment details to avoid thermal bridging. The constructors kept a log and photographic archive of all openings in the external building fabric. The MVHR system extracts air from the kitchen and bathrooms, reclaiming about 90 per cent of the heat in winter, to pre-warm incoming fresh air, which is supplied to the living-room and bedrooms – air is extracted straight to the outside in summer.

Space heating requirements are estimated to have reduced by 86 per cent, from 16,696kWh/year to 2,241kWh/year, which should reduce the tenant's heating bills considerably. A conventional wet radiator system with a condensing gas boiler was installed, after options such as heat pumps and underfloor heating were found unfeasible. The gas-condensing boiler also supplies hot water, but is supplemented by solar thermal panels installed on either side of the pitched roof, facing east and west, which should supply at least half of the tenant's hot-water requirements. Additionally, photovoltaic panels were mounted on the flat roof of the rear extension, to bridge the electricity supply shortfall to achieve the 80 per cent target – all electric lighting is LED.

Water conservation was implemented by installing 2.6/4ltr dual-flush cisterns to the two bathrooms, aerated taps and 'eco-shower' handsets. Conventional rainwater harvesting was rejected in this instance as being unfeasible with an underground tank and header tank pump. However, consideration was given to a simple gravity-fed rainwater-harvesting system, which uses a 300ltr filtered tank located about the stairs, which could supply nearly all of the water needed for flushing lavatories, based on the average rainfall in this location.

The financial savings to the tenant's are of equal importance to the reductions in carbon emissions, and energy consumption should reduce by 65 per cent, saving the residents several hundred pounds a year. Hyde Housing Association is ensuring that tenants understand how to live in the house with induction training, monitoring the performance of the dwelling, and conducting post-occupancy reviews to gain feedback from occupants.

Hyde House – external render system detail.

CHAPTER SUMMARY

- The Greeks and Romans used solar architecture to heat their homes. Vitruvius recommended that houses should face the sun to benefit from the warmth of the low winter sun.

- Thermal mass is the reason that stone constructions like cathedrals and castles are wonderfully cool and comfortable in summer. The thick, stone walls are able to absorb heat energy and store it to give it out again later during the cooler night. This heavy, thermal mass evens out the temperature to more comfortable levels throughout the day and night.

- Most old houses can be refurbished to reduce their carbon dioxide emissions by good management and improvements to controls, conservation heating, insulation, windows and doors, heating system and lighting. Zero carbon is a realizable goal with the addition of renewable technologies and low-carbon lifestyles.

- The rise of surburbia, and that most ubiquitous of British domestic forms, the semi-detached house, began with the increase in urban populations in the nineteenth century.

- About a third of Britain's dwellings were erected between 1800 and 1911 (several million houses), and a third of them between 1870 and 1911. Traditional domestic construction techniques did not change significantly over the period 1840–1919.

- Generally, houses built with solid walls need to 'breathe', as they will absorb moisture from rainfall but also release it through evaporation if the originally designed ventilation paths and construction techniques are retained. Most modern houses operate on quite different principles, as the introduction of the cavity wall in about 1920 started the change in construction technology to try to totally exclude moisture from dwellings and other building types.

- There are simple ways of improving the energy efficiency of all old houses, such as: improving building fabric by increasing thermal insulation and airtightness; improving windows by installing double glazing or secondary glazing; using efficient boilers and heating systems; better controls for heating and lighting; long-life, energy-efficient lightbulbs or LEDs; limiting excessive air infiltration by draught-stripping, bearing in mind the need for ventilation in many old construction types; better management of existing systems; undertaking effective preventive maintenance and repairs.

- Recent case studies have shown that properties of all ages, from Victorian to post-war dwellings, are capable of improvement to virtual carbon-zero targets, which reduce their carbon emissions by 80–90 per cent. Typical starting points are improving the building fabric with internal or external insulation, followed by improving airtightness and installing mechanical ventilation with heat recovery.

- Pressure tests are important to establish where the leaky areas of the existing building fabric are located, so that improvements are logically prioritized. Energy-efficient lighting, such as LEDs, is important to reduce electricity loads, capable of supply with appropriate on-site renewable energy technologies, such as photovoltaic panels. Solar thermal collectors pre-heating water and rainwater harvesting with simple systems are feasible in urban locations.

CHAPTER 4

New Houses

We are currently in a twilight war against climate change; we have identified the enemy, we are marshalling our forces and we are skirmishing; but within fifteen years we will be in all-out war against climate change, and it will influence everything we do.

Colin Challen, MP (2007)

DEFINITIONS

What exactly do we mean by the zero-carbon house, and is it really possible for us to design, construct and operate zero-carbon houses? The UK Government has proposed a number of definitions, over the years, starting with the Energy Efficiency Best Practice programme (EEBPp) in the 1990s, who proposed the following:

- Zero CO_2 = 100kWh/m^2/year (2 tonnes of CO_2/year).
- Zero heating = 50kWh/m^2/year (1 tonne of CO_2/year).
- Autonomous = 25kWh/m^2/year (0.5 tonnes of CO_2/year).

The more recent aspirations to require all new homes to be zero carbon from 2016 onwards, have further fuelled the debate over the definition of what a zero-carbon house is. In a recent consultation document, the UK Government has defined a zero-carbon house as one in which there will be net zero carbon dioxide emissions over the course of a year, after taking account of:

- emissions from space heating, ventilation, hot water and fixed lighting;
- expected energy use from appliances;

- exports and imports of energy from the development (and directly connected energy installations) to and from centralized energy networks.

This definition envisages that the zero-carbon house must:

- be built to high levels of energy efficiency;
- achieve at least a minimum level of carbon reductions through a combination of energy efficiency, on-site energy supply and/or (where relevant) directly connected low carbon or renewable heat; and
- choose from a range of (mainly off-site) solutions for tackling the remaining emissions.

This proposed definition is certainly sensible in its emphasis on energy efficiency, i.e. reducing energy demands, before concentrating on forms of on-site renewable energy solutions. As the visible and symbolic image of sustainable development, many potential house clients will invariably hold strong opinions on supply-side technologies, such as heat pumps, wind turbines, solar panels and biomass boilers – but the fact that they may not be necessary to achieve a zero-carbon or autonomous house rarely seems to occur to them. The provision of a range of expensive on-site renewable energy sources will also, surely, encourage the profligate use of energy, rather than the necessary emphasis on reducing energy demand through energy efficiency, lifestyle choices and behaviour.

However, others maintain that the zero-carbon house is an impossibility and that there can be nothing other than the zero space-heating house, at best. This position is maintained from the point of view of all the embodied energy that goes in to the manufacture of materials and components for a house, not to mention the energy expended in the construction process and so on. Complete carbon neutrality is a difficult claim to audit and quantify, leading many to posit that the zero-carbon house should be defined by its operation, over its lifetime of at least sixty years – if that can be carbon-free it is sufficient for the definition of the zero-carbon house. Although there is the possibility that the autonomous house, connected to the

electricity grid, could export enough energy back to the grid to achieve complete carbon neutrality over the lifecycle of its existence.

The question of embodied energy, and the energy and labour that goes into the construction of a house, is a compelling argument for the retention and improvement of the existing housing stock as the most energy-efficient form of property development. Conversely, detailed auditing schemes are having the effect of moving a number of new houses towards the Passivhaus Standard. This is defined as a dwelling that requires no separate heating system, which loses heat at no more than half-a-degree Celsius over a 12-hour period. Such stringent standards have been achieved in built houses in Central Europe, Scandinavia and Canada for many years, and are increasingly being built in the UK. Passivhaus standards certainly encourage care and attention to design details, to ensure that the fabric is airtight and that thermal bridges are minimized or eliminated, but the Standard relies on mechanical ventilation with heat recovery to minimize heat losses in winter. This often leads to a specialized debate over the amount of electricity needed to power the heat-recovery systems, which somewhat academic in the context of insulation and airtightness standards in the UK at present.

NEW AUTONOMOUS HOUSE

Site and Location

Brenda and Robert Vale designed and built an update of their 1970s autonomous house concept in the early 1990s and dubbed it the New Autonomous House. The site, in the centre of Southwell in Nottinghamshire, England, was purchased in 1991 for £69,000. Southwell is a small market town between Nottingham and Doncaster with a population of several thousand, and the site is in a conservation area within sight of the Norman Minster. The location and context obvi-

New Autonomous House, Southwell – west elevation.

ously demands the appearance, at least, of a traditional architectural approach, unlike the nearby rural site of the Hockerton Housing Project, which was also designed by the Vales. This challenge also shows that zero-carbon houses do not have to appear radically different from conventional homes and can fit in to historically sensitive areas, employing load-bearing brick walls and a clay pantile roof.

Accommodation and Funding

The New Autonomous House could claim to be the first autonomous house in the UK in the early 1990s, designed, as it was, to be environmentally friendly, self-sufficient in energy and water, treat its own wastes on-site, and to offer a healthy indoor environment to its inhabitants. The house is a two-and-a-half storey detached dwelling and consists of a habitable floor area of about 170m^2, with a total floor area of 290m^2, including the cellar and con-

servatory. The external building fabric embodies a low maintenance philosophy, with no exposed timber apart from the window frames, so that it boasts a 500-year design life. Long life and low energy to reduce whole-life costs are fundamental principles of sustainability. The house cost around £155,000 to build, which is very close to the typical cost of a house in the UK in the early 1990s, at about £540/m^2. The total cost of the project, at around £250,000, including land and professional fees, was funded with a conventional mortgage and built by a local builder.

Materials and Planning

The embodied energy of materials specified for the house was carefully assessed to minimize environmental impacts, starting with the foundations, which rest on old brick rubble from demolished buildings. The energy intensity of materials was

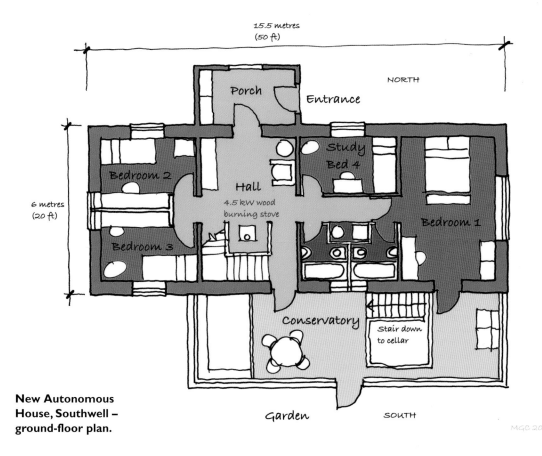

New Autonomous House, Southwell – ground-floor plan.

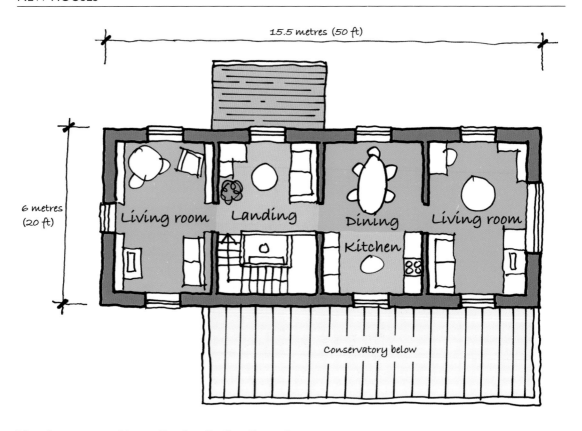

15.5 metres (50 ft)

6 metres (20 ft)

Living room   Landing   Dining   Living room

Kitchen

Conservatory below

New Autonomous House, Southwell – first-floor plan.

MGC 2009

Composting Lavatories

The water-closet is a cosseted symbol of Western civilization and often serves as a touchstone for progress but, in environmental terms, it is a continuing disaster. A more ecologically damaging system of disposing of human waste is difficult to imagine, as it effectively wastes fresh water – one of our most precious resources. The concepts of sustainability and zero-carbon living do not really entertain the idea of waste. In fact, the very word 'waste' has no translation in many cultures, as even our bodily wastes are perceived as what we give back to the earth. Although the argument of hygiene is where water-closets originated from, and centralized sewage systems in overcrowded conurbations undoubtedly reduce waterborne diseases in the population, we have to question the sense in using a third of the fresh water delivered to the average house to flush away our bodily by-products.

The water-flushable toilet consumes and pollutes large amounts of water, as well as generating 20 million tonnes of sewage sludge each year in the UK – a figure that equates to the total for all other household rubbish. All of this has to be pumped back and forth and treated, which uses vast amounts of energy. Nor is it entirely hygienic, as flushing can create splashes and bio-aerosols that contain human pathogens, which are avoided by composting toilets. The recycling of the ultimate product of the composting loo, back on to the land, is time-honoured and still treasured in many cultures. A recent experiment at the Centre for Alternative Technology (CAT) in Wales, which involved fertilizing winter onions with diluted urine, proves the point – yields were threefold the weight of the untreated control batch of the crop!

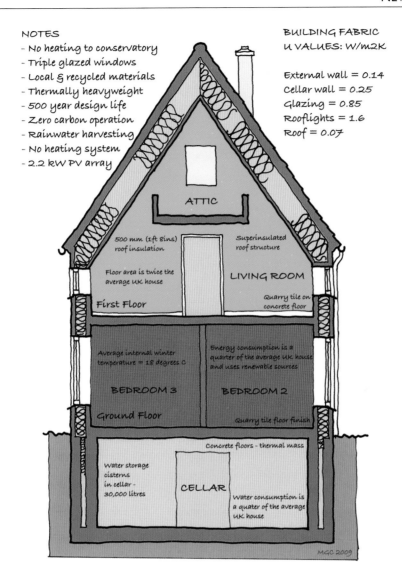

NOTES
- No heating to conservatory
- Triple glazed windows
- Local & recycled materials
- Thermally heavyweight
- 500 year design life
- Zero carbon operation
- Rainwater harvesting
- No heating system
- 2.2 kW PV array

BUILDING FABRIC
U VALUES: W/m2K

External wall = 0.14
Cellar wall = 0.25
Glazing = 0.85
Rooflights = 1.6
Roof = 0.07

ATTIC

500 mm (1ft 8ins) roof insulation

Superinsulated roof structure

Floor area is twice the average UK house

LIVING ROOM

First Floor

Quarry tile on concrete floor

Average internal winter temperature = 18 degrees C

Energy consumption is a quarter of the average UK house and uses renewable sources

BEDROOM 3

BEDROOM 2

Ground Floor

Quarry tile floor finish

Concrete floors - thermal mass

Water storage cisterns in cellar - 30,000 litres

CELLAR

Water consumption is a quater of the average UK house

MGC 2009

New Autonomous House, Southwell – cross-section.

extended to local sourcing, following the simple logic that the heaviest materials, such as the bricks, should come from sources closest to the site, thereby reducing the transportation impacts of the development. This was particularly important as the design strategy called for high thermal mass, which is best obtained from the heaviest of materials, such as brickwork and concrete. Such traditional construction techniques meant that the house contains about three times the total thermal mass of conventional UK masonry houses. Conse-

quently, the house is built using a load-bearing cavity wall construction, avoiding energy-intensive or toxic materials, while using as much waste and recycled materials as possible. Traditional in appearance, it is clad in red brick to match the architectural context.

However, the internal planning of the house is unconventional in that it is an 'upside-down' house, with the bedrooms and bathrooms on the ground floor, while the kitchen, dining and living rooms are on the first floor. The attic storey contains a gallery,

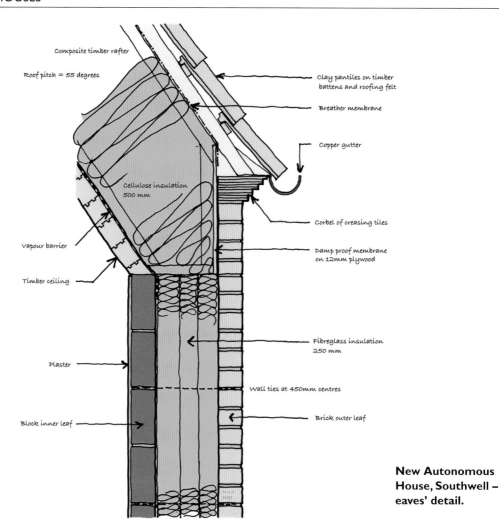

Composite timber rafter

Roof pitch = 55 degrees

Clay pantiles on timber battens and roofing felt

Breather membrane

Copper gutter

Cellulose insulation 500 mm

Corbel of creasing tiles

Vapour barrier

Damp proof membrane on 12mm plywood

Timber ceiling

Fibreglass insulation 250 mm

Plaster

Wall ties at 450mm centres

Block inner leaf

Brick outer leaf

New Autonomous House, Southwell – eaves' detail.

mezzanine space, a few metres wide that runs the length of the house, used as a workspace, library and store. Inspired by the plan of Southwell Minster, the architects also sought to plan the house in regular bays so that components, such as beams and purlins, were identical spans to optimize materials and cost. Turning the interior space planning upside down was a response to the specific site, as it raises the 'living spaces' above the dense perimeter planting and allows more daylight to penetrate them. Coincidentally, this type of upside-down planning is also a radical response in energy efficient houses, as heat rises to the areas that are occupied for most of the time. The house is super-insulated with 500mm-thick insulation in the roof.

Environmental Services

As the house is located in the centre of a town, within easy reach of mains' servicing infrastructure, the house is plumbed into the water and sewage system, as well as telephone and electricity. But as demonstration hybrid, the house is capable of complete environmental servicing autonomy, which shows a lower cost and environmental alternative. The cellar contains the autonomous environmental services, such as rainwater storage tanks and sewage composter for the waterless

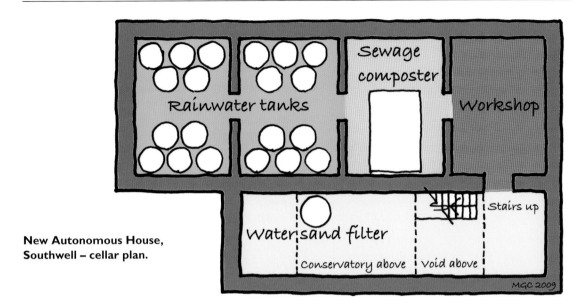

New Autonomous House,
Southwell – cellar plan.

composting lavatory. Rainwater is harvested from the roof of the house and conservatory, and stored in twenty recycled Israeli orange-juice tanks in the cellar, where it is filtered through gravity sand-filters. The composting lavatory obviates the need for water-borne sewage and allows human waste to be treated on-site to create dry compost that can be used to fertilize tomato plants grown in the conservatory or used on the garden. Water-use in the house was a fraction of the 150ltr per person average in the typical UK home, at just 34ltr per person each day.

The definition of an autonomous house is that it has both no need for space heating (zero heating) and is also zero carbon dioxide (no net CO_2 emissions in use). The New Autonomous House is super-insulated to the extent that no heating system is needed, with the exception of a small, wood-burning stove (4.5kW) in the entrance hall to provide psychological comfort. Passive heating is provided by the southerly facing, unheated conservatory. Electricity needs are roughly half that of a comparable UK household and are supplied by a 20m^2 array of photovoltaic panels, placed independently of the house, on a timber frame in the garden – at a slope of 45 degrees and facing due south. This 2.2kW system is also capable of exporting electricity back to the National Grid.

New Autonomous House, Southwell – view
from the garden.

Monitored Energy Use

The New Autonomous House shows the dramatic reductions that are possible through initial environmentally sensitive construction, energy-efficient operation and renewable energy supply. It uses about a quarter of the energy of a conventional house in the UK, and two-thirds of that is from renewable energy sources – if the planned heat pump was installed, it would be a completely zero-carbon house. As it is, it demonstrates a 95 per cent reduction in domestic carbon dioxide emissions compared to a conventional UK household. Space-heating energy use at 8.5kWh/m^2/year is a fraction of the average UK house (260kWh/m^2/year) and compares favourably with other low-energy houses around the world – about less than half of some of the examples in Germany and Switzerland, and less than a quarter of those in Canada.

Occupancy

There is no doubt that living in a zero-carbon house demands commitment and flexibility in lifestyle standards, compared to what we might regard as current living standards. The New Autonomous House contains a limited range of electrical appliances and a cold-wash washing-machine – there is also no freezer or dishwasher. As there is no heating system, apart from the symbolic wood-burning stove, average winter indoor temperatures in the living rooms are about 18°C, rather than the low 20s temperatures that people have become used to in their shirt-sleeves. But the re-radiation from the thermally massive construction helps to improve comfort conditions. Additionally, tenants have also successfully lived in the house, apart from the original designers and owners, who would be expected to have a vested interest in good performance of the house in-use.

Living in a super-insulated, passive-solar house, without a central heating system undoubtedly requires some adjustment, but is more in tune with nature, as testament from a comparable house in Germany shows. The occupants were subjected to a period of eighteen foggy days without sun in winter when indoor temperatures fell consistently below the predicted 18°C limits, and as low as 15°C for brief periods: 'It was too cold in the house but still bearable. Our tea consumption increased – a very efficient form of the interior heating – and we went to bed earlier than usual. This made it very clear to us that the house was completely dependent on the sun. Having to wait for the sun was an unusual but valuable experience in a world in which we are accustomed to getting everything we want immediately'.

Wood is Wonderful

Biomass is the term used for a wide variety of organic material, such as fast-growing trees (e.g. willow and poplar for woodchips), waste and recycled wood, straw and other waste organic matter. Biomass already represents the majority of the UK's renewable energy supply (about 1.5 per cent of UK primary energy supply). Clearly, a suitable and reliable source of biomass fuel is required to consider this renewable energy option for domestic use, such as coppicing from a nearby forest. On a micro-scale, a stand-alone, wood-burning stove provides space heating for a room, and can be fitted with a back-burner to give hot water. Central heating and hot-water provision require a larger system, with a boiler usually fuelled by logs, chips and wood pellets. Stand-alone room-heating equipments cost a few thousand pounds and running costs vary depending on the type of fuel used.

Historically, the good news is that wood warms you three times: when you cut and extract it; when you split and store it; and finally when you carry and burn it! One cubic metre of growing tree takes a cubic metre of carbon dioxide out of the air, stores a quarter of a kilogram of carbon and gives off three-quarters of a kilogram of oxygen through photosynthesis. Consequently, deforestation is a bad thing! One kilogram of dry wood has an energy content of about 5kWh (enough energy to heat two baths, or three small ones!). The best types of firewood are oak, ash, birch, hawthorn and hazel.

An energy-efficient house with a space-heating energy use of around 75kWh/m^2/year will need 5–6 tonnes of seasoned wood a year, requiring about 2 hectares (5 acres) of well-managed woodland. The Clean Air Act was introduced in the UK in 1956, shortly after the 'Great Smog' in London in the winter of 1952, which killed about 4,000 people. Over the period of a week in December 1952 the population was exposed to high levels of particulate pollution, exacerbated by the smoke from open, domestic coal fires. London is often still called the 'Big Smoke' as a consequence. However, wood fires can still be burned in smokeless zones if the wood-burning appliance has an exemption certificate or an authorized fuel source.

LIGHTHOUSE

Overview

The Lighthouse was the UK's first new house to meet Level 6 (the highest level) of the Code for Sustainable Homes, with a score of just over 90 credits. All new houses in the UK will have to achieve Level 6 by 2016. The Lighthouse achieves net zero-carbon status, with a prefabricated system of construction made of environmentally friendly materials and super-insulation. The form of the house is driven by a 40-degree roof pitch, which carries a large array of photovoltaic panels (4.7kW, 46m^2), while the efficient building envelope reduces heat loss to just a third of a conventional house. The prototype project was a collaboration between construction firm Kingspan, Sheppard Robson Architects and engineers Arups. Other sustainable technologies employed in the house include a biomass boiler, mechanical ventilation with heat recovery and water efficiencies to halve the consumption when compared to standard dwellings. The prototype is being monitored at the BRE Innovation Park in Watford, England.

The Lighthouse is a 93m^2 two-and-a-half storey, two-bedroom house, centred around an open-planned, top-lit, double-height living space. Bedrooms are on the ground floor, allowing for flexible living spaces above that are slotted between the overall timber portal frame. The external building fabric uses high-performance structurally insulated panels (SIPS) to reach U-values of 0.11W/m^{2}K for the walls and triple-glazing to reach 0.7W/m^{2}K for the windows, with high levels of airtightness. The ratio of glazing to external wall area is nearly half that of a conventional house, at 18 per cent, to reduce heat loss from windows – this factor induced the 'upside-down' house planning, so that rooflighting could be used for daylight and ventilation. The glazed wind-catcher feature on the roof induces cool air into the heart of the house. Materials are specified to minimize embodied energy, such as the sweet chestnut cladding, while selective thermal mass is also provided.

Lighthouse, zero carbon prototype house.

TOP LEFT: **Lighthouse – living spaces.**

TOP RIGHT: **Lighthouse – viewed from the south-west.**

MIDDLE LEFT: **Lighthouse – detail of ground-floor external cladding panel.**

BOTTOM RIGHT: **Lighthouse – attic study looking down to lounge.**

Renewable Energy

Energy needs, which are minimized through energy efficiency and efficient building envelope measures, are supplied from sources of renewable energy, such as the array of photovoltaic and solar-thermal panels on the south-facing roof, which eliminate an electricity bill and reduce the bill for space and water heating to about £30 a year. A 2kW biomass boiler, which is automatically fed with wood pellets, provides winter space-heating and is located in the utility/drying room, which obviates the need for an electric tumble-drier.

Water consumption is reduced to a maximum of 80ltr/person/day due to a number of water-saving features, which include rainwater collection from the roof (stored in a 1,200ltr underground cistern) for use in the washing machine and garden, and greywater recycling from the shower and bath for WC flushing. The latter has a dual-flush system of 6 or 4ltr per flush, while spray taps and shower heads are regulated to 2 and 6ltr/min, respectively – the

bath is also small! A-rated efficient white goods, such as a dishwasher that uses only 10ltr per use and a washing-machine that uses only 45ltr per use, further reduce water-consumption.

RENEWABLE HOUSE

The Renewable House is so called because it is almost entirely made from renewable materials such as a timber frame, Hempcrete walls and sheep's wool insulation. Hempcrete is made from hemp and lime mortar, and hemp is a commercial agricultural crop that absorbs CO_2 while it is growing. This house reaches a standard of Level 4 of the Code for Sustainable Homes from using these materials in its fabric alone, for an economic build cost of £75,000, excluding foundations and utility service connections. The prototype design for a three-bedroom house by Archial Architects can be extended into a semi-detached or terraced format to achieve economies of scale. Upgrading

---

Water Everywhere

Nearly three-quarters of the planet is covered in water, but 97 per cent of it is salt water and 2 per cent of it is ice at the polar caps, leaving only 1 per cent of fresh water, one of our increasingly precious resources. We are using about 70 per cent more water today than we did forty years ago in the UK, and global population has doubled over the same space of time. A bath can use around 80ltr of water, while a shower uses half as much. One flush of the toilet can use 10ltr, while washing machines and dishwashers can use over 50ltr a time. Using a hose-pipe to water the garden can use several hundred litres in an hour, which explains why hose-pipe bans are a regularly increasing feature of summer life in the UK.

A few per cent of fresh water that is supplied to the average house is used as drinking water, while around 95 per cent of it ends up down the drain – a third of that literally flushed away. Among one of the more alarming modern trends is the vogue for expensive bottled water, approaching the same price per litre as petrol. Those who leave the tap running while brushing their teeth are wasting about 10ltr of fresh water

each time. On average we use about 160ltr of fresh water a day each in the UK. Water efficiency begins with behaviour and fans of the 'Focker films' will remember Dustin Hoffman's immortal lines, which displayed his green credentials: 'If it's yellow let it mellow, if it's brown flush it down'! Many of the world's population survive on 10ltr of water a day, but we flush that away in one flush – dual-flush systems and 'hippos' to reduce the capacity of older cisterns could halve that.

The average house could collect 85,000ltr of rainwater a year on its roof, which is enough to fill nearly 500 water butts with free and natural water for the garden. A dripping tap is a travesty of waste for the sake of changing a washer. We also use vast quantities of water in manufacturing and industrial processes, such as nearly half-a-million litres to produce a small car, while1ltr of petrol to power it uses 70ltr to produce. Even a bicycle uses 150ltr of water in its manufacture. Simple interventions, such as installing water-efficient appliances and spray taps and showers can reduce your consumption by a quarter. Save water – it's a precious resource.

ABOVE: **Renewable House – entrance elevation.**

BELOW: **Renewable House – detail of ground floor and wall construction.**

ABOVE: **Renewable House – living space viewed from the kitchen.**

BELOW: **Renewable House – kitchen.**

Micro-Combined Heat and Power (CHP)

Combined heat and power (CHP) uses the heat from the generation of electricity for space-heating purposes, and is cost-effective in building types such as hospitals, because they are continuously occupied with a consequent need for continuous space heating in the heating season. Micro-CHP units for domestic use are now available and give each household the potential to become mini-power stations, also potentially eliminating the large transmission losses usually associated with supplying electricity from large power stations. Micro-systems are usually powered by gas and produce electricity and heat from the single fuel source. Many micro-CHP units are based on the Stirling external combus-tion engine (patented in 1816), which has a sealed system and uses an inert working fluid, such as helium or hydrogen. They are dissimilar to internal combustion engines and are no noisier than an ordinary boiler.

Domestic CHP units vary in size from half a kilowatt upwards and currently cost a few thousand pounds. As electricity is only generated when there is a demand for heat, other supplies of electricity are usually required – unless linked to batteries or fuel cells to store electricity for use when the CHP unit is not running. Mass-produced CHP units should reduce in price in due course, and are worth considering when replacing boilers – payback periods of a few years are possible.

the environmentally conscious features of the house, such as adding photovoltaic panels to the roof, enables Levels 5 and 6 of the Code for Sustainable Homes to be achieved. The prototype is being monitored at the BRE Innovation Park in Watford, England.

The continuous nature of the wall construction allows for high levels of airtightness and minimizes cold-bridging, while the Hempcrete gives U-values of $0.19W/m^2K$ with high levels of thermal mass – when I visited the prototype house on a hot summer's day with temperatures in the high twenties, the interior of the house was noticeably cooler, by several degrees Celsius. The high-performance timber windows are triple glazed to give U-values of $1.3W/m^2K$. Active technologies include a heat-recovery ventilation system, air source heat-pump and an underground heating system.

Construction time for the Renewable House is rapid, with the prototype taking only three months to build – the timber-frame structure took one week to erect, with a further four days required for the casting of the Hempcrete walls, which are initially sprayed on to the timber frame. The manufacturers estimate that if just 1 per cent of UK's agricultural land were used to grow hemp, it would produce enough to build 180,000 Renewable Houses each year. Despite the modest price and compact plan, the house is designed for flexibility and includes a downstairs bathroom.

Micro-Hydro

Micro-hydro usually means electricity generation levels of less than 100kW, using naturally flowing watercourses, such as rivers and streams. Clearly, unlike many other sources of renewable energy, micro-hydro is capable of continuous generation – in the absence of a drought. Energy demand is likely to be low when water flow is reduced in the summer. The scale of the potential micro-hydro scheme is dependent on the 'head' of water available (the height of water that provides pressure to drive the turbine) and the water-flow rate, which depends on the size of the watercourse and local rainfall. A typical domestic micro-hydro scheme costs several thousand pounds per kilowatt, £20,000 to £30,000 for a 5kW scheme. Economies of scale could result in a cost of a few thousand pounds per kW for larger schemes supplying a few hundred houses.

BIRMINGHAM ZERO-CARBON HOUSE

Overview

New-build houses tend to provide a focus for attempts to devise the zero-carbon house, ranging from outlandish architecture with a technological bent to more down-to-earth vernacular approaches. The development of new prototypes is important and legislation for mandatory zero-car-

TOP: **Birmingham House – street elevation.**

BELOW: **Birmingham House – garden elevation.**

bon houses in the UK applies only to new-build, but new homes are a small fraction of the total stock, a few per cent. As approximately 35 per cent of UK energy is used in homes and over 80 per cent of existing houses will still be in use beyond 2050, a small number of new homes will be insufficient to reduce carbon emissions dramatically. The existing housing stock is crucially important for our efforts to reduce carbon dioxide emissions in the built environment, and they can be architecturally exciting with an element of new interventions. The Birmingham Zero-Carbon House is perceived by many as a vision of the future for our approach to the existing housing stock, and it achieves Code Level 6 of the Code for Sustainable Homes.

The architect, John Christophers, set himself a threefold target when compiling the brief for the refurbishment and extension of his Victorian terrace house in the outskirts of Birmingham, England. He wanted to create a zero-carbon house that achieved Code Level 6 of the Code for Sustainable Homes, to upgrade his 170-year old house to the same standards as new energy-efficient houses and to act as an inspiration to others by showing that, through the use of exciting spaces, daylight and materials, so-called 'green architecture' is not dull. It was a challenging brief but there is little doubt that Christophers has pulled it off, certainly judging from the hundreds of visitors who flock to see the house on open days.

Birmingham House – ground-floor plan.

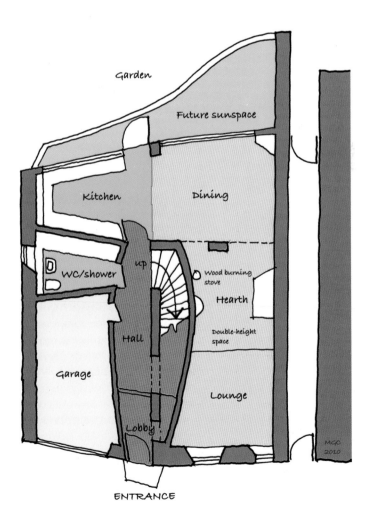

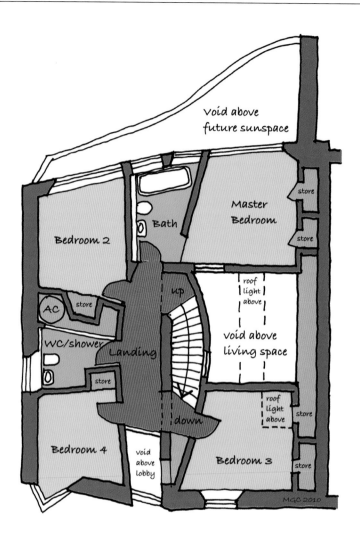

The Birmingham house refurbishes and extends an 1840, two-bedroom terraced house to create a four-bedroom house with a studio loft. The original floor area is more than doubled (from 50 to 110m^2) for the modest price of just over £1,000 per square metre, while retaining immaculate environmental credentials that make this the first Code Level 6 retrofit in the UK. It is a unique melding of old and new to create a zero-carbon house, in which dozens of reclaimed materials were used. While the re-use of existing housing is laudable, the artistic extensions and additions also show that green architecture does not have to be dull.

Planning and Materials

The extension enlarges the existing house by extending on to vacant space to the street frontage, doubling the space on ground and first floors, and adding a long, top studio. The studio roof is at the required height, pitch and orientation for electric (PV) and hot-water solar power to provide 90 per cent of the house's renewable energy needs. The open-plan design of the ground floor creates a variety of different spaces, including a tall, top-lit living room. Full-height glazing to the garden (and a future glazed sun space) maximizes useful winter solar gains, while a mature ash tree shades the glass in summer. An internal garage retains the secure off-road car-parking space.

Town planners welcomed the modern ecological design, filling a gap site. The new dormer and first-floor bay window interventions relate to the roofscape of surrounding Arts and Crafts houses. The high-level projecting dormer-window frames the wide view north to the city centre of Birmingham. The original Victorian house is extant at the front. Reclaimed brick and white render pick up the dominant local building materials on the exterior facades. External joinery and cladding is from local and untreated sweet chestnut lathes. Natural building materials are used throughout the interiors. The planning permission application was made in September 2007 and construction was from October 2008 to November 2009. An open book AEC contract was negotiated, as the design and construction innovations made a fixed-price tender impossible.

The three-storey, unfired, clay-block, load-bearing structure of the new extension is probably a UK first, and provides very low embodied energy with high thermal mass (better than concrete or brick); its hygroscopic properties regulate internal humidity. Rammed earth floors are implemented throughout, undulating softly and finished with beeswax. Combined with the solid, brick walls of the original structure, very high levels of thermal mass are provided throughout. The architect considers this the simplest, least expensive way of ensuring the house will not overheat in the predicted hotter summers that climate change will inevitably bring. This approach contrasts starkly with the modern methods of construction (MMC) and social housing requirements for largely lightweight, prefabricated buildings.

Walls are finished in traditional naturally coloured lime plaster, with a slight sparkle of ground recycled green glass aggregate. Recycled glass is also used for kitchen worktops and wet-room floors. The unlacquered brass ironmongery, designed by Arne Jacobson, is also reclaimed. The top-lit, radiating stair is compressed between

Birmingham House – design model.

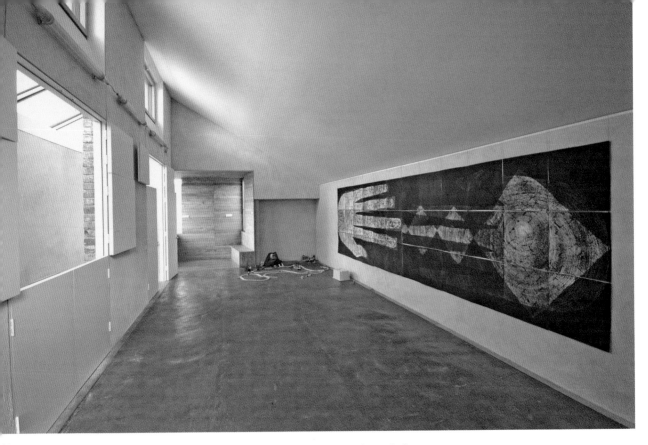

Birmingham House – top-floor studio with rammed earth floor.

Birmingham
House –
stairwell.

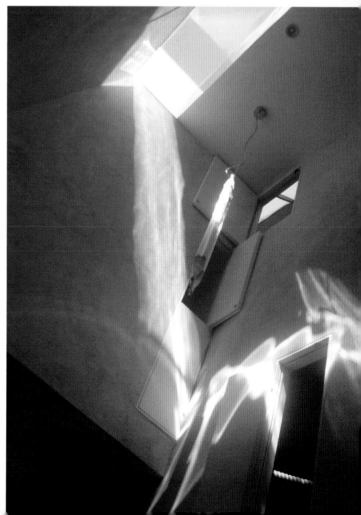

existing brickwork and new, gently curved, enclosing walls, while natural hemp is used for handrails. Canadian honeydew maple boarding (200 years old) was reclaimed from a demolished local factory floor. The recycled maple was used for stair treads, an internal shuttered balcony, kitchen, window seats and the complete lining of the top-floor timber dormer.

The first floor has a study and three bedrooms, with shuttered openings overlooking the double-height living area. The shutters may be closed (introvert) or open (extrovert) to give extra daylight and assist natural summer ventilation. High-quality natural daylight is achieved throughout the house with four rooflights and various windows with mirrored reveals. The mirrors intensify the daylight and bounce sunlight deep into the rooms. The lobby screen and landing floor use composite honeycomb core panels to reflect extra daylight. Airtightness is essential for very low energy design. Advice and a system of membranes and accessories for achieving this were imported from the Republic of Ireland, as they were not available in the UK. The scheme achieves more than ten times building regulation standards and uses mainly recycled newspaper insulation.

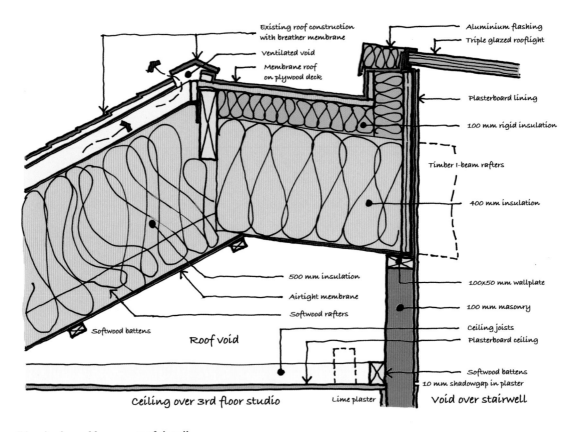

Existing roof construction with breather membrane

Ventilated void

Membrane roof on plywood deck

Aluminium flashing

Triple glazed rooflight

Plasterboard lining

100 mm rigid insulation

Timber I-beam rafters

400 mm insulation

500 mm insulation

Airtight membrane

Softwood rafters

100x50 mm wallplate

100 mm masonry

Ceiling joists

Plasterboard ceiling

Softwood battens

Roof void

Softwood battens

10 mm shadowgap in plaster

Ceiling over 3rd floor studio

Lime plaster

Void over stairwell

Birmingham House – roof detail.

Sustainability

Electricity, space and water-heating are all net zero-carbon renewable energy, with no fossil fuels used. Insulation, airtightness, ventilation, passive solar design, water, lighting, waste, transport, materials, social engagement and site ecology are all addressed in response to the Code Level 6 categories. The U-values achieved are: wall = 0.11, roof = 0.08 and windows (triple-glazed) = 0.65W/m²K. A mechanical heat-recovery ventilation system serves every room for winter use, reclaiming up to 93 per cent of waste heat, with mixed-mode natural ventilation in summer. The high thermal mass of the structure and natural stack ventilation in the atrium allow night cooling for the predicted hotter summer temperatures.

Water conservation is achieved by harvesting rainwater from the roof and storing it in a 2,500ltr cistern in the old cellar, which serves WCs, the washing-machine and a dedicated kitchen tap. Low water use fittings and 4/2.6ltr WC cisterns are specified, reducing water usage to 80ltr per person per day. There is no increase in surface water run-off from the development, and a gravity-fed greywater harvesting system allows bathwater to be used in the garden. Excellent daylighting is provided to all habitable rooms with mirrored linings to some rooflights and windows, including some translucent floor areas. Low-energy lights, induction hob and A++ electrical appliances are used throughout. The house has full waste, recycling and composting facilities, and virtually all of the site construction waste was recycled.

ABOVE: **Birmingham House – translucent floor.**

BELOW: **Birmingham House – wood-burning stove.**

Renewable sources of energy include 9m² of evacuated tube solar hot-water collectors, which have an estimated annual yield of 5,150kWh; 36m² of solar electric PV panels, which have an estimated annual yield of 3,500kWh; and a 7kW high-efficiency clean-burn woodstove, which provides top-up heating and hot water for the coldest weeks of the year. An 850–1,000ltr cylinder at first-floor level collects and stores heat from the solar panels and stove. Bird boxes and bat boxes are built into the house to increase biodiversity on the site. Finally, the project has engaged on a number of levels to act as an educational showcase, which has included several open days that attracted several hundred people each. Dissemination has included visits from local primary school children, including a joint project based on renewable energy and recycled materials with a school and visiting artist. Extensive media coverage is also ensuring that the project is widely disseminated.

ONE EARTH HOUSE

Overview

One Earth Houses were built as part of a much larger new housing development called Upton Square in Northampton, England in late 2009. They are a response to the Code for Sustainable Homes, by famed British eco-architect Bill Dunster, who was recently awarded an OBE for his contribution to sustainable housing design. The initial development constitutes a terrace of six houses, but there are plans to extend the typology so that it constitutes roughly a third of the overall development. The houses were the first in the UK, as part of a speculative housing development, to reach Code Level 6 for the Code for Sustainable Homes – as such they are zero-carbon luxury homes, even without the planned roof-mounted wind-turbines, which were not yet implemented in late 2009.

Philosophy

Bill Dunster has worked tirelessly to bring about zero-carbon houses, since envisaging solar-powered housing estates as an architectural student at Edinburgh University. His dream became reality at the Beddington Zero-Energy Development (BedZED), a housing estate for the Peabody Trust in South London, at the turn of the twenty-first century. He has continued his quest just north of the capital city, claiming that the One Earth Houses will go beyond Code Level 6, to reach an off-the-scale standard of his own invention, if the windmills are added – Code Level 7! Dunster believes that cheap fossil fuel supply is now very limited and that peak demand, where global supplies are insufficient, will be reached by the year

ABOVE: **One Earth Houses – south elevation, with solar panels on the roof.**

BELOW: **One Earth Houses – north elevation, with sedum roof.**

2020. His position is thoroughly researched and the evidence he produces during frequent and fierce email debates, involving other members of the RIBA Sustainable Futures Committee, is invariably irrefutable. If he is right, this leaves us just one decade to redesign every aspect of our lives, and work towards sustainable, zero-carbon living.

Implementation

The development in Northamptonshire is the result of decades of experience in designing low energy houses by Bill Dunster Associates Architects, which now consists of a well-tried and tested approach. Energy demand is minimized by a combination of passive and active means, starting with a carefully balanced specification of materials and orientation to maximize passive solar gains; although the houses are made of a timber frame, this is rendered thermally massive by lining walls

and ceilings with eco-concrete, which stores solar heat gains during the day. The houses are designed with super-insulation so that they do not need a conventional heating system, with hot water supplied from the solar thermal panels mounted on the roof. Similarly, electricity demand is supplied from the roof-mounted photovoltaic panel array. They are the first open-market Code Level 6 homes in the UK, which are available for rent, shared-ownership and for sale – they were built for approximately 10 per cent more capital costs than conventional houses.

Passive Solar Design

The Upton Square zero-carbon houses are designed with a large, south-facing double-height sunspace, which absorbs heat from the sun before it enters the main house. On sunny days the sunspace heats up like a traditional greenhouse, but opening the internal doors allows this heat to dissipate throughout the house. This solar gain is particularly useful in winter, spring and autumn – but at the height of summer, the large, roof overhang and yellow, retractable awnings, reminiscent of an historic shopfront, provide shade, which, along with the high thermal mass of the fabric, prevent summertime overheating. The thermal mass of the houses stores heat during the day and releases it back into the house during cooler nights – creating a continuously stable internal temperature. The houses are super-insulated with 300mm of insulation to minimize heat loss, which is about three times the thickness of a conventional house.

Water

Rainwater is harvested from the roof and channelled into an underground tank where it is sand-filtered before being pumped up to a header tank for storage. This unpurified water is used for flushing lavatories, watering the garden and washing electric cars – not to mention watering the sedum and other wild flowers on the green roof, which covers the north roof. Water-saving appliances are

One Earth Houses – detail of south elevation.

**One Earth
Houses – detail
of wind cowls.**

used throughout the houses, such as a 2/4ltr dual-flushing toilet, and aerated taps, which use reduced amounts of water with a stronger flow. A++ rated white goods also reduce water and energy use. The 300ltr, dual-coil, hot-water tank stores enough water for the whole family all day.

Internal Environment

Living in a zero-carbon, passive, solar house requires some adjustments in order to make sure that it works as intended, and some monitoring of resource-use, but the benefits in terms of cheaper running costs and one-planet living are obviously worthwhile, and ultimately essential to our sustainability. Additional economic benefits can be obtained by selling surplus electricity to the National Grid. Airtight construction and heat recovery to minimize heat loss also require great care in the specification of internal materials such as paints, finishes and fittings to ensure that they are not toxic – so that they do not give off noxious 'off-gases'. The contemporary architectural interpretation of the domestic chimney is present in the wind cowls, a time-tested feature of Dunster's eco-architectural approach, that allow passive ven-

tilation with heat recovery. The wind cowls supply the houses with fresh air and extract stale air, without any energy use, while pre-warming the incoming air from the stale air with a heat-exchanger.

DENBY DALE PASSIVHAUS
Overview

Jeff and Kate Tunstall wanted to build an energy-efficient and cost-effective retirement home in their garden in West Yorkshire, and decided to follow the Continental 'Passivhaus' system. They employed the services of a local architect from Huddersfield, Derry O'Sullivan, with veteran eco-engineer Peter Warm supplying specialist energy consultancy. The location demanded a traditional, cavity wall construction with an outer leaf of local stonework, to satisfy the town planners that the dwelling was 'in-keeping'. Getting the design right and within the modest budget of £141,000 for a 120m², three-bedroom house took some time, with the initial L-shaped design with a conservatory failing to meet the stringent Passivhaus standards. Further modelling, using the Passivhaus planning package (PHPP) software, resulted in a

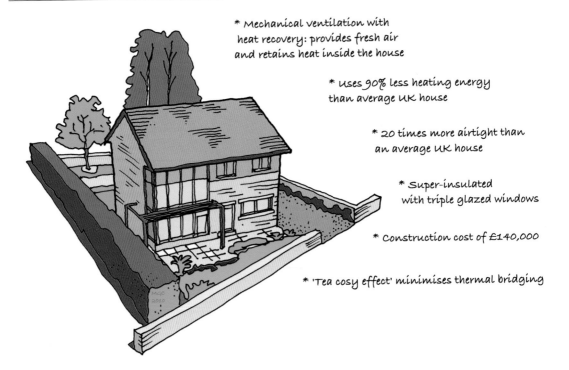

* Mechanical ventilation with
heat recovery: provides fresh air
and retains heat inside the house

* Uses 90% less heating energy
than average UK house

* 20 times more airtight than
an average UK house

* Super-insulated
with triple glazed windows

* Construction cost of £140,000

* 'Tea cosy effect' minimises thermal bridging

ABOVE: **Denby Dale Passivhaus – view from the south.**

BELOW: **Denby Dale Passivhaus – ground floor plan.**

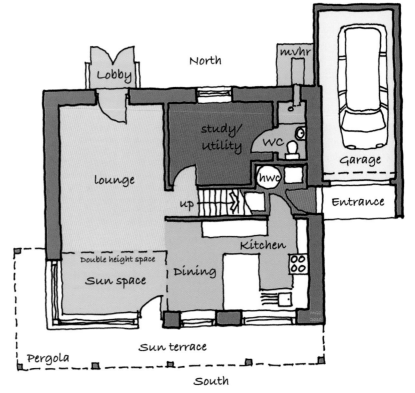

**Denby Dale Passivhaus
– first floor plan.**

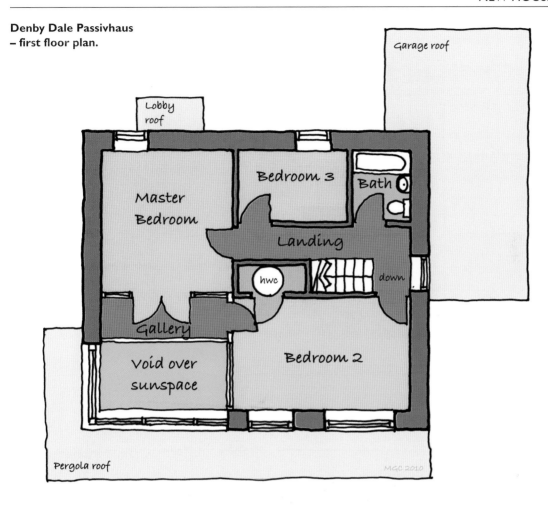

rectangular planning footprint, with the long side oriented north/south.

The more compact rectangular, almost square, plan footprint proved more economic and energy efficient, and met the obligatory 15kWh/m²/year space-heating requirements (UK average is almost ten times this figure), with expected annual heating costs of about £75/year. The Tunstall's desire for a conservatory was integrated into the plan as a sun space, with external shading to exclude high-summer sun angles. In line with the Passivhaus approach, the house is super-insulated with stringent airtightness and a mechanical ventilation system with heat recovery. The Denby Dale Passivhaus has an airtightness of 0.33 air changes per hour at 50Pa of pressure (Passivhaus certification requirements are 0.6 air changes/hour).

Passivhaus Standard

Passivhaus buildings are usually built with a timber-frame construction or solid, concrete, blockwork walls with external render. Cavity wall construction was chosen for this zero-carbon house, as it was more familiar to British builders and the materials were easily sourced from local building merchants. The house should be the first certified Passivhaus dwelling in the UK using a cavity wall construction. Additionally, masonry construction, such as cavity walls, provides a high degree of thermal mass, which helps to keep internal temperature stable in winter

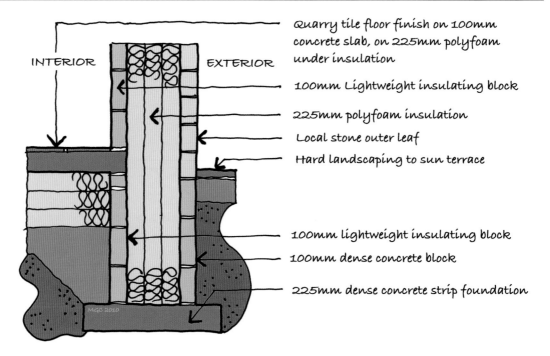

INTERIOR   EXTERIOR

Quarry tile floor finish on 100mm concrete slab, on 225mm polyfoam under insulation

100mm Lightweight insulating block

225mm polyfoam insulation

Local stone outer leaf

Hard landscaping to sun terrace

100mm lightweight insulating block

100mm dense concrete block

225mm dense concrete strip foundation

Denby Dale Passivhaus – detail section through cavity wall.

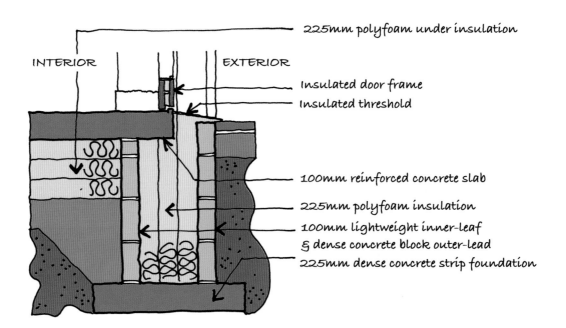

INTERIOR   EXTERIOR

225mm polyfoam under insulation

Insulated door frame

Insulated threshold

100mm reinforced concrete slab

225mm polyfoam insulation

100mm lightweight inner-leaf & dense concrete block outer-lead

225mm dense concrete strip foundation

Denby Dale Passivhaus – detail section through cavity wall and threshold.

and summer. This house shows how Passivhaus construction can be achieved inexpensively by a small, skilled, construction team.

Unfortunately, according to the Code for Sustainable Homes (CfSH) assessor for the house, Jim Parker, houses built to the high Passivhaus standard, such as this, may only meet CfSH Level 3/4 criteria. Parker goes on to claim that the carbon savings achieved by the Passivhaus approach are not accurately reflected in the CfSH assessment system. He also thinks that some houses that receive up to Level 6 actually perform worse in terms of airtightness and space heating, but gain points in other areas, and sometimes through the use of inefficient and expensive bolt-on renewable technologies. The Passivhaus approach demands great attention to detail and workmanship on-site to achieve construction airtightness and to eliminate thermal bridging and other heat losses.

CHAPTER SUMMARY

- Definitions of zero-carbon houses vary. The UK Government's definition from the 1990s defined a zero-carbon house as one that used 100kWh/m^2/year (2 tonnes of CO_2/year) of energy; a zero-heating house used 50kWh/m^2/year (1 tonne of CO_2/year) of energy; and an autonomous house used 25kWh/m^2/year (0.5 tonnes of CO_2/year) of energy. Current UK definitions include a house that has net zero carbon dioxide emissions over the course of a year; a house built to Code Level 6 of the Code for Sustainable Homes; and a house built to the Passivhaus Standard.
- All zero-carbon houses must start with emphasis on energy efficiency, i.e. reducing energy demands, before concentrating on forms of on-site renewable energy solutions. The provision of a range of expensive on-site renewable energy sources will also, surely, encourage the profligate use of energy, rather than the necessary emphasis on reducing energy demand through energy efficiency, lifestyle choices and behaviour.
- Complete carbon neutrality is a difficult claim to audit and quantify, leading many to posit that the zero-carbon house should be defined by its

operation, over its lifetime of at least sixty years – if that can be carbon-free, it is sufficient for the definition of the zero-carbon house.
- The embodied energy and the energy and labour that goes into the construction of a house is a compelling argument for the retention and improvement of the existing housing stock, as the most energy-efficient form of property development.
- The New Autonomous House was designed by the architects Robert and Brenda Vale in the early 1990s in Southwell, Nottinghamshire. Its location in a conservation area demands that the house has a conventional appearance. This was the first autonomous house in the UK, designed as environmentally friendly, self-sufficient in energy and water, treating its own wastes on-site, and offering a healthy indoor environment to its inhabitants.
- The internal planning of the New Autonomous House is unconventional in that it is an 'upside-down' house with the bedrooms and bathrooms on the ground floor, while the kitchen, dining and living-rooms are on the first floor. It contains no heating system apart from a small wood-burning stove. It also contains a composting lavatory and rainwater harvesting.
- The embodied energy of materials specified for the New Autonomous House was carefully assessed to minimize environmental impacts. The design strategy called for high thermal mass, which is best obtained from the heaviest of materials, such as brickwork and concrete. Such traditional construction techniques meant that the house contains about three times the total thermal mass of conventional UK masonry houses. The house is super-insulated with cavity walls and 500mm-thick insulation in the roof.
- The Lighthouse was the UK's first new house to meet Level 6 (the highest level) of the Code for Sustainable Homes. All new houses in the UK will have to achieve Level 6 by 2016. The Lighthouse achieves net zero-carbon status, with a prefabricated system of construction made of environmentally friendly materials and super-insulation. The form of the house is driven by a 40-degree roof pitch, which carries a large

array of photovoltaic panels (4.7kW, 46m^2), while the efficient building envelope reduces heat loss to just a third of a conventional house. Other sustainable technologies employed in the house include a biomass boiler, mechanical ventilation with heat recovery and water efficiencies to halve the consumption when compared to standard dwellings.

- The Renewable House is so-called because it is almost entirely made from renewable materials, such as a timber frame, Hempcrete walls and sheep's wool insulation. Hempcrete is made from hemp and lime mortar. This house reaches a standard of Level 4 of the Code for Sustainable Homes from using these materials in its fabric alone, for an economic build cost of £75,000, excluding foundations and utility service connections. Upgrading the environmentally-conscious features of the house, such as adding photovoltaic panels to the roof, enables Levels 5 and 6 of the Code for Sustainable Homes to be achieved.

- The Birmingham Zero-Carbon House is perceived by many as a vision of the future for our approach to the existing housing stock, and it achieves Code Level 6 of the Code for Sustainable Homes. The Birmingham house refurbishes and extends an 1840, two-bedroom terraced house to create a four-bedroom house with a studio loft. Rammed earth is used for the internal walls and floors, which provides very low embodied energy with high thermal mass, while its hygroscopic properties regulate internal humidity. Electricity, space and water-heating are all net zero-carbon renewable energy, with no fossil fuels used. Water conservation is achieved by harvesting rainwater from the roof and storing it in a 2,500ltr cistern in the old cellar, which serves WCs, the washing-machine and a dedicated kitchen tap.

- One Earth Houses were built as part of a much larger new housing development called Upton Square in Northampton in late 2009. They are a response to the Code for Sustainable Homes, by famed British eco-architect Bill Dunster. The houses were the first in the UK, as part of a speculative housing development, to reach Code Level 6 for the Code for Sustainable Homes.

- The Denby Dale Passivhaus is one of the first houses in the UK built to the Passivhaus standard, which uses super-insulated cavity walls and mechanical ventilation with heat recovery (MVHR) to reduce heat losses in winter. The more compact plan footprint meets the obligatory 15kWh/m^2/year space heating requirements, with expected annual heating costs of about £75/year.

CHAPTER 5

Earthships

I am more taken by one who lives the truth than by one who speaks it ... we are like a lizard eating itself by starting with the tail; eventually the damage starts to outweigh the nourishment.

Michael Reynolds (1989)

EARTHSHIP HISTORY

Earthships are so-called because they are autonomous and self-contained dwellings that are metaphorically afloat on land, in a similar way to which a ship at sea has to provide all the necessities of life to sustain its crew on a long voyage – an earthship does the same on land. They are the brainchild of maverick American architect Michael Reynolds, who goes so far as to claim divine inspiration for their original conception in the form of dreams he experienced decades ago. He claims that they are 'independent vessels to sail on the seas of tomorrow'.

Earthships have distinctly counter-culture beginnings in the desert of New Mexico, near Taos, where Reynolds still lives and spent decades experimenting with his concept of the ultimate environmentally sustainable house. The original beginnings in the 1970s were as much about opting out of the consumer society, while building a house without mortgage payments and utility bills, largely

---

Bottle House History

There is a long and venerable history of building houses from waste materials, such as bottles, particularly in the USA. This dates back to the early 1900s in states such as California and Nevada where supplies of more usual building materials, such as timber, were in short supply. The more famous examples include Tom Kelly's bottle house in Rhyolite, Nevada, which is now a ghost town. Rhyolite was a boom mining town in 1906 when Kelly, a saloon owner, built his bottle house out of 50,000 used beer, whisky, soda and medicine bottles. He is reputed to have built the house in six months when he was 76 years old – it is now a tourist attraction. An even earlier bottle house, dating back to 1902 but demolished in the 1980s, was William F. Peck's bottle house in Tonopah, Nevada. It was a four-square and robust structure built out of 10,000 beer bottles, with an architectural feature of contrasting, square-shaped bottles around the doorway. These were Jhostetter's Stomach Bitters bottles, a product that was mainly alcohol mixed with about 10 per cent opium – guaranteed to take the upset tummy blues away! Western pioneer-town settlers made use of the most abundant building materials available, which were usually the empty alcohol bottles from the first commercial structure in the settlement – the saloon!

Earthships in the Greater World Community, near Taos, New Mexico, USA.

out of the waste material from that very throw-away society, as autonomous living. There is a large contingent of earthsailors, under the auspices of the Greater World Earthship Community, near Taos NM, where Reynolds now has a state licence for an 'experimental environmental housing site', after much legal wrangling, which included losing and then regaining his state licence and federal credentials to practise architecture.

Earthships have gradually entered the mainstream and there are many of them built, and being built, around the globe, applying the basic, if radical, principles embedded in the earthship concept to different climatic regions. There is at least one earthship in every state in the USA, which covers a wide range of climates in itself. There are earthships in Europe, South America and Japan. Michael Reynolds still frequently travels the globe with an 'earthship crew' to drop anchor with a new, pioneering earthship at each port-of-call. The first earthship in the United Kingdom was built in

Scotland at Kinghorn Loch in Fife, completed in 2004, followed shortly afterwards by another, much larger one, just to the north of Brighton. A third is currently under construction in Scotland, at Wishaw near Greenhead Moss. The UK examples have obtained planning permission as educational showcases with regular tours run by enthusiasts for members of the public. Dozens of earthships have appeared all over Europe, from Normandy and Belgium to Norway and Spain, many of which are open to the public or available for holiday hire, while others are private, autonomous dwellings.

The earthship concept is undoubtedly an extreme aspiration of treading lightly on the earth and being completely self-sufficient, off-grid and more or less free of the follies of the modern, consumerist society. They originally involved self-building a mortgage- and utility bill-free dwelling, created largely from the earth on the site and the waste of modern civilization. Now there are package and pre-built varieties available, as the concept

ABOVE: **Earthship Fife at Kinghorn Loch, Fife, Scotland, UK – built in 2004.**

BELOW: **Earthship Brighton, near Stanmer House, Brighton, UK – built in 2005.**

becomes more commercial – somewhat ironically? They can claim to be truly carbon-zero houses. The concept can be taken as hardlined, as Reynolds would like it to be, or in a slightly more diffused way, as the late American actor Dennis Weaver, who commissioned a large earthship in Colorado from Reynolds, which is quite ironically expansive in its floor area and even includes a separate guest suite 'earthship'. However, there is no doubt that such celebrity patronage is good for the dissemination of the sustainability concept, at least. Reynolds has now more or less standardized the concept and off-the-peg plans for rectangular or circular earthships, with technical specifications, and power and water modules, can be purchased from his website.

The claim is that earthships heat and cool themselves naturally, collect their own power from the sun and wind, harvest their own water, produce their own food and treat their own sewage on-site. Reynolds also starred in the recent documentary film *Garbage Warrior*, which tells the tale of the early beginnings, recent political wrangling and environmental disaster missions to establish prototypes of sustainable living in the developing world. The title is indeed apt, as some of Reynold's original structures were constructed from a patented 'brick' of several aluminium cans, wired together, before he broke away from the strictures of a conventional 'brick' to use the garbage more directly to build sustainable dwellings.

Discarded rubber tyres, which shamefully make up one of the primary ingredients of most landfill around the world, are among the prime materials for an earthship, making up the retaining wall for the earth berm (a raised earthen area), raked at an angle of 8 degrees. The tyres are filled with dense earth, ritualistically pounded into their rims with sledge hammers (labour costs are typically half of the total budget), to ensure a core of high thermal

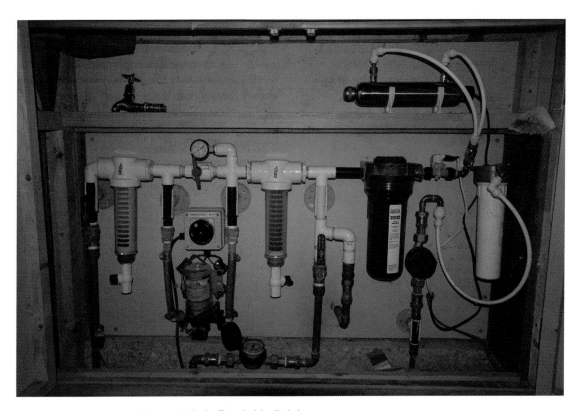

WOM or water organizing module in Earthship Brighton.

mass, to the traditional New Mexico finish of adobe or earth plaster to the internal and external walls. This finish is also hygroscopic (absorbs and releases water vapour) to stabilize the relative humidity of the interiors – earthship owners report no misting of mirrors in the bathroom. Artistic touches include the incorporation of recycled and myriad-coloured glass bottles to provide modest borrowed daylighting into internal areas, such as bathrooms.

TOP: **Detail of recycled tyres from Earthship Brighton.**

BELOW: **Recycled coloured glass bottle wall in the shower room of Earthship Brighton.**

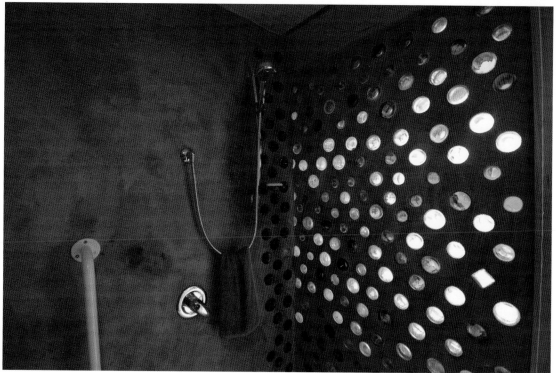

Michael Reynolds – American Eco-Tect

Michael E. Reynolds is the charismatic inventor of earthships, and he is, by turns, called a 'maverick, bad boy of architecture' and 'eco-hero'. Equally feted and frowned upon by the architectural establishment, Reynolds initially followed a conventional architecture training and graduated from the University of Cincinatti in 1969. His final-year thesis was published in *Architectural Record* magazine in 1971, and looked at making architecture out of unconventional materials. From those early beginnings his rhetoric has become little short of messianic, after nearly four decades of practical research into earthships. He contends that earthships can help more people to simply survive in an uncertain future, while wider introduction of the concept could change the reality of that future, and firmly states that 'if humanity is to survive, they will have to do something like this'.

His moment of epiphany came when he realized that the garbage or waste from a throw-away, consumer society could be recycled and used as building materials. In the early 1970s he set about putting his thesis into practice in the desert of New Mexico, where he built the Thumb House (1972), so-called because it looks like a cocked thumb in profile, with a glazed promontory poised for solar gains. This early house was constructed from 'bricks' made of several aluminium beer cans each, wired together and laid in a conventional fashion with mortar to form walls that were plastered over. This recycled 'brick' design was awarded a US patent in 1973. The oil crises of the early and mid-1970s stimulated a fresh look at the resources that went into architecture and saw the rise of solar architecture, with its emphasis on dense construction to form thermal mass to stabilize internal temperatures. The search for thermal mass led Reynolds to the ultimate throw-away material: the car tyre, which, when full of pounded earth, amounts to a great deal of thermal mass, indeed. Combined with an insulation wrap, this forms his 'ideal wall'.

The main driver behind Reynolds's self-styled environmental revolution was that conventional architecture and construction were so wasteful of resources. He now calls his approach 'biotecture'. He evolved the earthship concept over four decades of experimentation, but it was not all plain sailing. In some cases, the architecture was so experimental that clients were sometimes dismayed at the range of functional performance.

Reynolds is not surprised that he has encountered more than occasional opposition from bureaucracy as, to put it in his own words, he is 'building buildings out of garbage and running sewage through the living room'. However, after such a long evolution, the earthship concept is now entering the mainstream, within the increasing imperatives of global warming and climate change. Reynolds has gone from losing his state licence to practise architecture, to being invited to address the American Institute of Architects.

It also helps when celebrity actors, such as the late Dennis

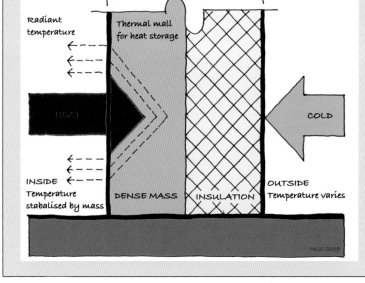

TOP INSET: **Michael Reynolds.**

BOTTOM LEFT: **Ideal wall.**

Weaver and Keith Carradine, have commissioned Reynolds to design and build top-of-the-range earthships. As there is nothing like a celebrity endorsement to popularize an idea these days, and quite deservedly so in this case, we can only hope that zero-carbon living will become as popular an aspiration as many other celebrity-fuelled pursuits. Reynolds, quite loftily, sees earthships as organic units that allow the cyclical use of resources, rather than the conventional linear process that produces waste – 'a water-producing, heat-producing, food-producing organism that coexists with and sustains the human organism'.

The recent documentary film called *Garbage Warrior*, directed and filmed by Oliver Hodge over three years, during which time the debut director allegedly re-mortgaged his house to fund the project, has undoubtedly given an inspirational and popular boost to earthships. One was even featured recently on the UK home improvement TV programme, Channel Four's *Grand Designs*. The *Garbage Warrior* film is an 84-minute drama, which quickly consolidates from disparately hippy beginnings into a mesmerizing journey to save humanity from itself. Reynolds, clearly revelling in his messianic role, forsakes his favourite pastime of pounding earth into tyre rims, and takes on the politicians of New Mexico, to establish his legal right to continue his architectural experiment on a grander scale. One memorable scene involves a Republican senator's assertion that 'You can't prove global warming with science... it's a myth'.

However, the final words must be given to Reynolds, who describes one of his latest earthships, called the Phoenix, as 'There's nothing coming into this house, no power lines, no gas lines, no sewage lines coming out, no water lines coming in, no energy being used... we're sitting on 6,000 gallons of water, growing food, sewage internalized, 70°F (21°C) year-around... what these kinds of houses are doing is taking every aspect of your life and putting it into your own hands... a family of four could totally survive here without having to go to the store'. Conversely, Reynold's view of present world ecology is best summed up by his analogy that 'We are like a lizard eating itself by starting at the tail; eventually the damage starts to outweigh the nourishment'.

THE SIX PRINCIPLES OF EARTHSHIPS

Thermal and Solar Heating and Cooling

The thermal mass of the massive earth berm structure of the back retaining wall, with dense earth pounded into the tyres, is one of the key concepts of the earthship. Tyres are a ubiquitous waste resource, the world over, and are easily harvested, providing a suitable and convenient receptacle for the thermal mass from the pounded earth. A small earthship uses as few as 200 tyres, while Dennis Weaver's two-tiered 'earth yacht' used a few thousand. This heavy structure provides enough thermal mass to stabilize the widest range of temperature swings, such as the highs of 40°C during the desert day to the −40°C of a winter desert night.

For a practical example of the effect of thermal mass it is only necessary to enter the thick, stone-walled interior of a cathedral, cottage or church during a hot summer's day, to feel the immediate cooling and comforting relief. The front of the earthship is designed in a configuration to maximize winter solar gain and exclude the high-summer sun angles that would cause overheating. A simple and common sense idea encapsulated in Reynold's words 'A dog lies in the shade in the summer time. He lies in the sun during the winter'. In temperate climates, the 'stack effect' of hot air rising to the open rooflights at the back of the earthship should provide adequate natural ventilation for comfort. In extremely hot climates, air is cooled by passing it through an earth tunnel, where it loses heat to the cool, thermal mass of the ground, before it enters the interior as cooler air.

Solar and Wind Electricity

Earthships obviously aim to dramatically reduce the need for energy use by using insulated thermal mass to stabilize winter and summer internal temperatures, and acquiring passive solar energy from low winter-sun angles, which is stored in the thermal mass. This strategy should obviate the need for heating systems in most climates, but a wood-

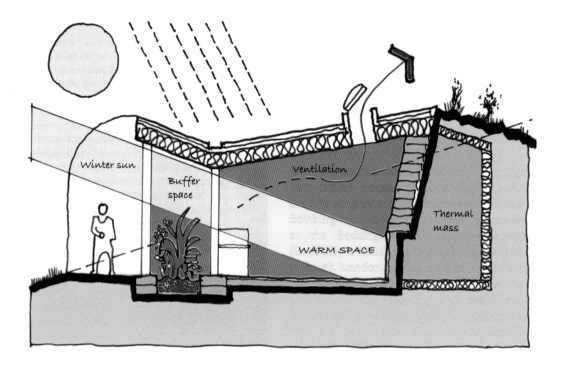

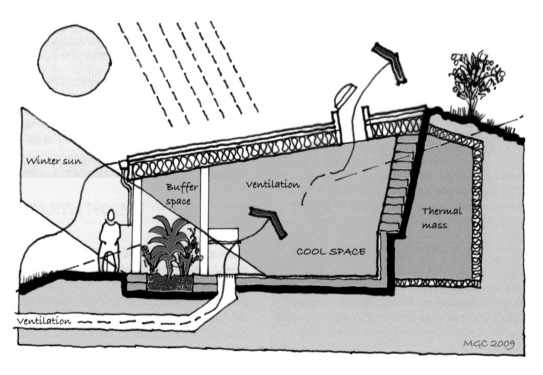

Cross-sections through earthships for cold climates (top), and hot climates (bottom).

POM or power organizing module in Earthship Fife.

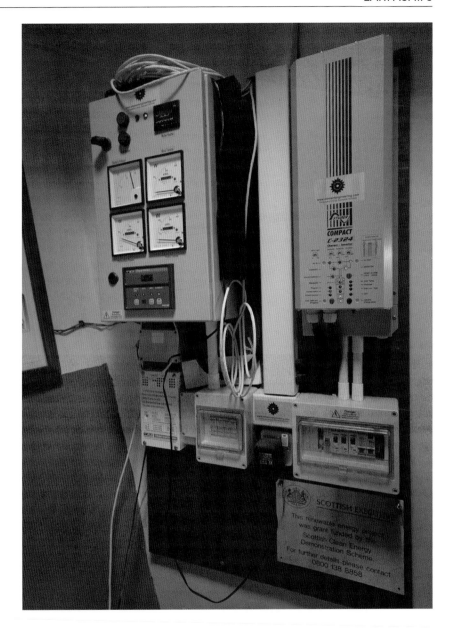

burning stove is usually included, for psychological as much as practical comfort. Wood is a renewable resource, and earthship electricity is also generated from renewable sources via photovoltaic panels on the roof and wind turbines, as appropriate. A combination of both wind and solar electricity should cover most seasonal variations – the solar panels will provide most of the supply in summer, while wind turbines (and hydro-power, if available) should take most of the demand burden in winter.

However, battery stores are essential to tide over lulls in natural supply and allow for the conveniences of a modern lifestyle, complete with essential appliances, but probably not running to the likes of dishwashers, apart from in celebrity earthships! The first principle should slash energy demand, while the second principle demands optimum 'system sizing' to be economical. A 'POM' or Power Organizing Module' regulates the electrical supply and includes a change controller, inverter and fuse box.

Contained Sewage Treatment

Reynold's contends that there should really be no such thing as 'waste water' – it is too much of a precious commodity. Given this sentiment it seems ironic that many earthships contain a water-borne sewage system at all, but the presence of a conventional water-closet or toilet does make the house less alien to most people. While earthships in arid regions commonly have a composting lavatory to save water, the water-borne system in other areas is an important part of the autonomous sewage system. This means that the earthship is not con-

nected to a mains' sewage system and does not need a septic tank. Sewage in an earthship refers to 'blackwater' from the toilet. Greywater from the sinks, shower and so on, are processed into the water-recycling system and eventually end up as blackwater. Greywater is typically about four-fifths of the waste water from a household.

All of the solids and waste water from the WC are treated by natural processes in what are known as the 'botanical cells' in an earthship. These are entirely sealed from the surrounding earth with an impervious liner to prevent seepage. An incremental system of filters is placed at the bottom of the cell, so that the sewage slowly seeps through the layers of rocks, gravel, sand and soil – with plants taking up the nutrients from the final layer of soil. The required size of the botanical cells is carefully calculated, but generally has a capacity of around 4,500ltr or 1,000 gallons.

Planter in the conservatory of Earthship Brighton.

TOP: **Detail of recycled tyre and aluminium can wall construction from Earthship Fife.**

BELOW: **Detail of recycled coloured glass bottle wall in the main room of Earthship Brighton.**

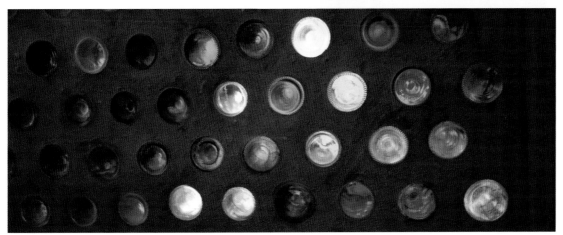

Natural and Recycled Materials

One of the fundamental touchstones of evolved earthships is the use of that ubiquitous and talismanic waste material of modern civilization – the rubber automobile tyre. Although many used tyres are recycled, re-used or burnt as fuel, many also went to landfill in the UK until this was recently outlawed by EU legislation. About 48 million waste tyres were generated in the UK in 2004. That such a symbolic waste material is the fundamental building block of an earthship has poetic resonance. However, they do work well as a receptacle for rammed earth, pounded with sledgehammers to painstakingly provide the immense thermal mass necessary for the earthship concept. No solar gain without pain! Heuristic and empirical experience suggests a 'batter' or rake of approximately 8 degrees from vertical to form the retaining walls of an earthship – just enough to satisfy the purist who insists on a minimum of parallel surfaces for organic architecture. Spaces between the tyres are filled with other waste materials, such as aluminium cans and plastic bottles.

One of the most visually appealing aspects of earthships is the use of coloured glass bottles in walls to give the effect of stained glass, in contrast to the general 'junk aesthetic' of the architecture. These are achieved by angle-grinding the necks off wine bottles and the like and attaching two together with duct tape. Earthship builders who are wholly in pursuit of the junk aesthetic will no doubt pride themselves in re-using and recycling as many components and materials, such as architecturally salvaged doors and windows and so on, so that they achieve a zero-embedded energy score for the building fabric of their earthship.

Detail of bottle construction for walls at Earthship Brighton.

Water Harvesting

Clean water is fast becoming a precious resource, leading Reynolds to quote a New Mexican water-well driller who predicted in a radio interview that 'The next world war will be fought over water', at the beginning of his book *Water from the Sky*. Earthships are not connected to mains' water infrastructure and rely on on-site supplies, usually from rainwater harvesting and melted snow captured on the roof and stored in a large water cistern. The theory is that enough water to survive is collectable in regions where rainfall is over 200mm a year (8in), which is most of the world apart from extreme deserts.

Water from the mains relies on mains' electricity for purification and pumped supply to you – it is better to have water-supply autonomy and be less of 'the problem' and more of 'the solution' accord-

ing to the earthship philosophy. Water conservation is the first step, as water usage varies widely from an average of a few hundred litres per person each day in Europe, to a profligate thousand litres in locations such as Las Vegas, Nevada. The average in North America is 575ltr/person/day (Lpd), and in the UK it is 150Lpd (half of this is used in toilet flushing, baths and sinks). It is 10Lpd in Mozambique – the minimum UN and WHO survival level is 20Lpd, for drinking and personal hygiene.

Water is also recycled in the earthship system: rainwater is harvested and purified to make it drinkable and useable for washing; the greywater waste is then used to water the internal planters in the conservatory; toilet flushing is the next use (although composting toilets can also be used to conserve water); and the final use is as 'blackwater' or sewage that feeds reed beds and plants to turn it back into harmless water. Rainwater storage is clearly crucial, especially in arid regions, and earthship water-storage tanks are typically 50,000–60,000ltr in capacity (this is larger by a factor of ten than most domestic rainwater-harvesting systems).

Water conservation is obviously a key concept of the earthship lifestyle, as aptly illustrated by the fact that water is frequently 'tankered' in to rented earthships in New Mexico, for visitors who are still in a water-profligate mode, and have not adapted to desert living. In more temperate climes, with higher rainfall, this combination of measures should make water autonomy within quite easy reach. A 'WOM' or Water Organizing Module is used to control water consumption, which includes a series of filters, ultra-violet treatment to kill bacteria and a water meter. I have drunk a glass of water from Earthship Fife and not only lived to tell the tale, but to write this book as well!

Food Production

Food production is an integral part of the earthship ideal, not least because the internal planters contribute to the other systems, such as the recycling and oxygenation of greywater. Food and flora is grown in the 'interior greywater botanical cells'. However, complete food autonomy would be difficult in the average-sized earthship, leading

The Trouble with Tyres

Automobile tyres are necessarily very tough, long-lasting and flexible. They do not biodegrade and are not easily recyclable, as the vulcanization of rubber is not a reversible process. Vulcanization is the chemical process of curing rubber, which involves high heat and the addition of chemicals such as sulphur – this improves the elasticity and durability of rubber, while making it resistant to chemical attack. Many other products, apart from tyres, are made with vulcanized rubber, such as shoe soles and rubber hoses. Bowling balls are made from hard vulcanized rubber, sometimes called ebonite or vulcanite.

Over 700 million new car tyres are produced in the world every year, and most of them are stored, buried or burned when they are worn out. Approximately 270 million tyres are thrown away, each day, in the USA, where they have a stockpile of 3 billion used tyres. The UK, alone, discards around 450,000 tonnes of used tyres each year. Landfill is where most used tyres end up, but this is not a safe method of disposal – toxic chemicals can leak out of them and contaminate water supplies; they make landfills structurally unstable; and they can catch on fire. A dump in Wales, containing 10 million tyres, caught fire in 1989 – it is still burning today. Sending used tyres to landfill sites was banned in the EU by a European Directive on 1 July 2006, but many tyres are illegally dumped, or fly-tipped, as it is known. There were fears that the new legislation would increase the amount of fly-tipping, and there were a number of incidents, such as the abandonment of eighteen 40ft-long containers of used tyres in Cheshire.

Current estimates put around a quarter of old tyres as re-used and half of them recycled in some form. That still leaves a great deal of used tyres in the world, and their use as a building material has to be top of the list. Other uses include re-treading them for further use, but this is decreasing due to the larger amount of budget tyres now on the market. Eco-fashionistas will find a pair of shoe soles made from used tyres irresistible, such as the Blackspot Unswoosher sneaker or plimsoll – the upper is made from organic hemp and the sole from recovered tyres. Items of stationery, such as pencil cases, mouse mats and notebooks are made from recycled tyres by The Remarkable Recycling Company in the UK – all products are labelled 'I used to be a car tyre'. This company recycles 80 tonnes of used tyres a year and even uses recycled cooking oils to fuel their manufacturing process. Some remaining uses include carpet underlay, playground surfaces, garden mulch and hanging one from a tree to make a swing!

Research at Leeds University by Dr Paul Williams, largely in response to the EU Directive, has looked into the process of pyrolysis to recover oil and gas from used tyres. Pyrolysis is not a new process, but has had little commercial value in the past. The old tyre is heated without oxygen, which breaks down its molecular structure and releases gas, oil and a residue solid called 'carbon black'. Carbon black can be used as a filler or colouring agent in composite materials, such as inks and paints. Dr Williams estimates that this process can recover about 20 per cent of the tyre's original price, even recovering the steel cord for scrap metal. However, until this process is perfected – build an earthship!

Reynolds to advocate the giving over of entire rooms to food production in larger earthships. But even if you could grow enough food for self-sufficiency, this assumes you are a vegetarian and can withstand a seasonal diet that could become somewhat monotonous in the depths of winter. Even the most die-hard environmentalists admit to occasional trips to the supermarket for variety, and they usually keep some livestock, such as sheep, pigs and chickens. Clearly, the earthship needs some external acreage and a suitable climate for livestock production to achieve tolerable food autonomy.

Although this risks straying into survivalist territory and the mentality that the *Mad Max* movies are documentaries of the future, food production is worthy of consideration on economic grounds alone. Food cannot remain a relatively cheap com-

WOM or water organizing module in Earthship Fife.

Case Study: Dennis Weaver's Earthship, Ridgway, Colorado, USA

Key Points

- 8,500ft^2 luxury home.
- Dream home called 'Sunridge'.
- Mostly powered and heated with solar energy.
- Monthly electricity bill of about $50.
- Rock-walled and solar-heated jacuzzi.
- 3,000 used tyres and 350,000 used aluminium cans used in construction.
- Recently valued at nearly $4 million.

General

That late actor and environmentalist, Dennis Weaver, who died in 2006, built a bespoke earthship to Michael Reynolds' designs in the late-1980s. In 1989 the Sunridge Earthship became Colorado's first and the largest one built to date. Dennis Weaver was probably best known to most worldwide TV audiences as 'McCloud' in the long-running and successful detective series of the same name. He was also a dedicated environmentalist who professionally produced a 30min film showing the building of his earthship, or 'earthyacht', and conveyed wider environmental messages. Weaver also founded the Institute of Ecolonomics (IOE) in 1993, whose mission is to demonstrate that a strong economy and a healthy ecology is the only formula for a sustainable future.

Dennis Weaver's Sunridge Earthship is located on a south-facing ridge in Ridgway's Pleasant Valley. It is set in a 20-acre estate amidst pine and cottonwood groves at the foot of the Rocky Mountains. Dallas Creek winds through the property into a private lake where wild geese abound, along with other wildlife such as llamas and deer. The mammoth earthship is set on two levels with a connecting curved staircase link built out of used aluminium cans.

modity in an era of rising oil prices, because it is invariably transported long distances to arrive at the point of sale – like all commodities its price is dependent on the cost of transportation. And the carbon-emission costs of air freighting out-of-season produce from the other side of the world is quite frightening, leading to an emphasis on local produce in the more enlightened supermarket chains. Anyone who has every owned and worked a small kitchen garden or allotment knows the satisfaction of producing some of their own vegetables, and the hard work entailed. Fresh, home-grown vegetables are usually incomparably superior in freshness and taste to those from a supermarket, where they are transported and stored in depots for some time before arriving at the point-of-sale. It is clearly possible and desirable to produce some food in an earthship, even if it is only fresh tomatoes in the greenhouse-like environment of the conservatory.

One of the recent earthships in Taos, New Mexico, called The Phoenix is designed by Michael Reynolds to provide for more expansive food production, with two additional greenhouses. About a third of the total floor area of Phoenix is given over to food production, including livestock such as fish, chickens and goats, the latter species also providing for the production of eggs and cheese.

TOP: **View of Earthship Weaver.**

BELOW: **Ground-plan of Earthship Weaver.**

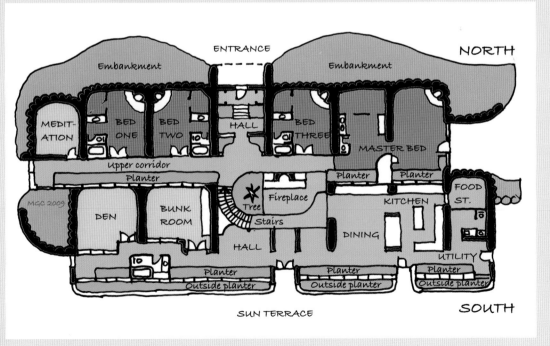

The main room of Earthship Fife.

Case Study: Earthship Fife, Scotland, UK

Key Points

- First earthship built in Scotland and the UK, opened in 2004.
- Education demonstration project run by a charity.
- Earthship concept successfully adapted to the local climate.
- 300 used-car tyres and 1,500 aluminium cans recycled into the construction.
- Renewable energy sources include hydropower, which supplies half of the electricity requirements.
- Contained sewage treatment is in external planters, which are covered because of the high rainfall in Scotland.

- Water is harvested into a 4,550ltr (1,000 gallon) water-storage tank buried beneath the earthship.
- The earthship is surrounded by agricultural land, which provides the potential for complete self-sufficiency in terms of food production.

General

The first earthship built in the UK is small but perfectly formed, at 31.5m² (315ft²). It was built as a demonstration project on a site besides Kinghorn Loch on the south coast of Fife in Scotland – as this is agricultural land, full planning permission was obtained for non-residential use in April 2001. A few months later, Michael Reynolds and an earthship crew from Solar Survival Architecture in New Mexico arrived to put in an intensive eight-day building programme to help Paula Cowie, the project manager, start the project.

Paula was inspired by a trip to The Greater World Earthship Community in New Mexico, during which she pounded her first used tyre with earth to help build an earthship. She returned to Scotland and made the application of earthships to her native land and climate the subject of a master's thesis, entitled 'Sustainable Earthships in Scotland: Are Earthships Viable?'. Needless to say, she concluded that they were and embarked on building the first one in Scotland and the UK, taking the words of Mahatma Gandi to heart: 'You must be the change that you want to see in this world.'

Earthship Fife took two years to complete and involved the labour of around 230 volunteers, working over weekends and work-experience days, and was finally launched on 21 August 2004. The building was initially given a five-year temporary building warrant, and there were concerns over the potential fire hazard of using old tyres in the construction – but it now has a permanent building warrant, which validates the approach in Scotland. Building standards for residential use were applied during the planning and building control processes. It now serves as an educational and research building, run by the Sustainable Communities Initiative (SCI), who are continuously monitoring the earthship's performance in Scotland's climate.

Thermal and Solar Heating and Cooling
Earthship Fife applies the same principles of passive solar heating and cooling that were used in the original earthships in New Mexico – immense thermal mass in the walls of earth-filled used tyres. The damp Scottish climate dictated the use of some cement to hold the damp adobe plaster finish of the walls together, and it obviously took longer to dry between layers than it does in the desert. The thermal wrap behind the walls is comprised of two layers of a permeable geotextile matting called Voltex (an ecological alternative to plastic), which sandwiches a layer of impermeable sodium bentonite granules. Voltex is robust, so it should last for a long time, but it is unfortunately heavy to work with on-site and it is also ten times as expensive as plastic. There are no active heating or cooling systems in the earthship.

Solar, Wind and Water Electricity
The addition of hydro-electric power from the nearby burn (stream) is an advantage of this particular location, where the lade (lade is the Scottish word for the flume or mill race that channels water from the source to the turbine) from the old mill that is 50m away was re-used. The hydro-turbine produces about half of the earthship's power (1,300kWh/year). A 600W Proven WT600 wind-turbine was installed on the hill behind the earthship, with a hub height of 5.5m – the site is good for wind, which averages 7.5m/s – it is on the Scottish coast! The wind-turbine produces 40 per cent of the power demand – about 1,000kWh/year. A 300W photovoltaic system mounted above the sunspace provides the remaining power demand of some 255kWh/year.

A 24V battery bank to store the renewable energy is mounted in a box on the roof (due to the lack of internal space), which stores about 18kWh to 80 per cent discharge, which would keep an average family home going for about two days. As Earthship Fife is a demonstration project with no-one actually living in it, it uses about 3kWh/day, so the stored energy should last six days if all other sources stop. This is unlikely as the stream alone should supply a minimum of 3.6kWh/day, even in summer – the earthship should never run out of renewable energy. The total capital cost of the renewable energy systems, controls and battery was about £12,500.

Contained Sewage Treatment
The sewage system was adapted from the original New Mexican designs to function in the wetter Scottish climate – there is no septic tank

Case Study: Earthship Fife, Scotland, UK (continued)

in the system. When the harvested and recycled greywater finally reaches blackwater stage, it nourishes plants in contained botanical cells, or blackwater beds. These are in the external planter beds, which are covered in Scotland because of the high rainfall. All sewage in the earthship is treated in this contained manner, with none entering the external environment. The system was accepted by the authorities as it was proven to work. Conventional treatment, of half a tonne of sewage each year from the average family, uses a great deal of energy and still has water-pollution risks.

TOP: **Aluminium can internal wall of the bathroom at Earthship Fife.**

BELOW: **Roofscape at Earthship Fife, which harvests rainwater – the battery box is to the left of the rooflight.**

Food production at Earthship Fife – including a plastic bottle greenhouse.

Natural and Recycled Materials

Earthship Fife obviously fully embraced the concept of using recycled materials, such as used tyres, bottles, aluminium cans and recycled timber; and natural materials, such as the earth that is excavated to create an earthship, natural paints and sheep's wool insulation. This can also make good economic sense, as 'rubbish' is usually free – and in the case of used tyres, the tyre disposal company should pay you to take away and 'dispose' of them. However, some natural materials are more expensive than 'conventional' ones, for example natural paint is twice as expensive as chemical paint, and sheep's wool is three times as expensive as fibreglass insulation. Budgets have to be balanced and donations were always welcome!

Water Harvesting

A butterfly-roof serves to collect rainwater, rather than the conventional pitched roof that sheds water. Water harvesting may seem superfluous in the wet Scottish climate, but water shortages are not unknown in rural and island areas in dry summers. And on-site harvesting in a rural location obviates the need for expensive mains' connections and infrastructure. Most rural Victorian properties had a water-storage cistern in the basement – as Earthship Fife does. A 4,550ltr (1,000 gallon) water-storage tank is buried beneath the earthship. Water is used and recycled until it reaches the blackwater stage, in line with the earthship approach.

Food Production

The sunspace of Earthship Fife only provides area enough for the cultivation of a few tomato plants, but it is surrounded by acres of agricultural land, not to mention the nearby loch with its natural fish stock and potential for fish farming. An earthship in this sort of rural loca-tion provides the potential to live the 'good life' of complete self-sufficiency. The blackwater botanical is located externally in a green-house made of reclaimed timber and plastic bottles, and there are also polytunnels for vegetable production.

Earthship Brighton's south-facing conservatory façade.

Case Study: Earthship Brighton, UK

Key Points

- Second earthship built in the UK and opened in 2006.
- Educational demonstration project run by the Low Carbon Trust (LCT).
- Earthship concept successfully adapted to the local climate.
- Renewable energy sources include solar, wind and biomass.
- Contained sewage treatment with a septic tank, reed bed and soakaway.
- Water is harvested into a 20,000ltr (4,400 gallon) water-storage tank buried beside the earthship.
- The earthship is surrounded by agricultural land, which provides the potential for complete self-sufficiency in terms of food production.

General

Earthship Brighton is much larger, over four times the floor area, than its predecessor in Scotland, at 135m² (1,350ft²). The earthship near Brighton was the first built in England, shortly after the first Earthship in the UK was built in Scotland. Both projects were self-built using a wide array of financial grants, sponsorship and donations. The large amount of labour to build an earthship, such as the sheer physical effort of pounding thermal mass into tyres, was provided by volunteers. The Brighton Earthship also benefited from help and leadership by Mike Reynolds and his international earthship crew. Misha Hewitt was the project manager and founder of the Low Carbon Network, who managed to raise the £280,000, which was the final cost of the building. Professional architects and engineers prepared the detailed drawings and structural calculations.

The single-storey building acts as a community centre for Stanmer Organics who lease land nearby to produce organic food. But even though not for residential use there were a number of regulatory hurdles to overcome. For example, the Environment Agency initially took a dim view of the idea of using old car tyres as they classify them as toxic waste. They were probably, understandably, worried that a dangerous precedent of disposing of used car tyres by building a wall and roof, and calling it a building, could be established. They finally relented after much lobbying. The building was started in April 2003 using skilled labour from members of the Low Carbon Network. There were a number of modifications to Reynold's New Mexico design for the English climate, such as the roof, which only needed to collect rainwater rather than snow, most of the time.

Foundations were not needed on the Brighton site as the ground is stable chalk. The rear retaining wall was initiated by simply laying a line of tyres on the ground. In the traditional manner these were filled with earth and the chalk dug out of the hillside to create a level site. The tyres are pounded with sledgehammers until they resembled over-inflated tyres. The tyre-retaining wall is also made more structurally stable by hammering vertical steel spikes through successive layers of tyres. The tyres are laid at a slight angle, of about 8 degrees, into the earth behind the rear wall.

There is about 2 metres of compacted chalk behind the rear tyre wall, enrobed in a layer of insulation and the damp-proof membrane, to isolate the thermal mass and prevent water seepage, respectively. The thermal mass of chalk acts like a storage heater, absorbing heat in the summer to keep the space cool and re-emitting solar heat gains during the winter. The rest of the building is a timber-framed structure, with a truss roof, and post and beams to the front elevation. The surface of the rear wall was plastered with an adobe mixture of earth and chopped straw. The floor slab used only about a third of the Portland cement necessary, as it was made from a mixture of magnesium oxide and cement – the manufacture of cement can be very energy intensive.

The general ethos of constructing a building out of rubbish was vigorously pursued, for financial reasons as much as philosophical or purist ones. One notable piece of opportunism was chancing upon a local undertaker who threw away waste granite every month, and a few skipfuls of this waste material make-up the mosaic floor to the sun-space. Similarly, the dwarf wall, which separates the main room from the atrium, is made from granite blocks scavenged from a company that was closing down. By 2005, the completely autonomous building, with only a telephone utility connection, was really taking shape, in spite of some funding problems that were overcome, and a range of renewable energy technologies were on-site, such as a wind turbine, photovoltaic and solar panels, and a biomass heater. A range of batteries stores enough power for the building to survive ten days in the absence of any wind or sun.

Thermal and Solar Heating and Cooling
Earthship Brighton applies the same principles of passive solar heating and cooling that were used in the original earthships in New Mexico – immense thermal mass in the walls of earth filled used tyres. Temperature monitoring over the first two years of operation showed that internal air temperatures in the main room of the earthship were, on average, some 2°C higher than the external air temperature. The average temperature in the main room was around 14.5°C, reaching a low of about 11°C in winter and a high of nearly 18°C in summer. The average temperature

Case Study: Earthship Brighton, UK *(continued)*

ABOVE: **Back of the main room at Earthship Brighton, with wood-burning stove in the corner.**

BELOW: **Solar thermal and photo-voltaic panels on the roof of Earthship Brighton.**

of the thermal mass fell steadily from November to March, as it was slowly dissipating heat to maintain a stable temperature in the occupied space. Energy stored in the wall increased from March to September. A wood-burning stove was installed in the main room, as much to provide a psychological hearth as a practical measure. This is a 15kW Extraflame stove that burns wood pellets from sustainable sources.

Solar and Wind Electricity

Earthship Brighton is not located near a source of micro-hydro power so relies on a large array of solar panels and a wind turbine for its renewable energy. The sizing of the renewables' system allows for the major provision of electricity needs from the photo-voltaic panels (1,116W Unisolar electric panels) in summer and the wind turbine (900W Whisper H40) in winter.

Power operating module (POM) and hot water cylinder at Earthship Brighton.

About 70 per cent of electricity requirements are supplied by the sun in summer and, conversely, by the wind in winter, with the other system supplying the remainder, by turns. Excess generation is stored in the battery system (46kWh capacity), which usually stores enough energy for at least ten days in the absence of any renewable generation, enough to keep the average family home going for five days. The total capital cost of the renewable energy systems, controls, batteries and biomass stove was about £28,000.

Contained Sewage Treatment

Earthship Brighton is not connected to the mains' sewage system, but it does have a 2,800ltr septic tank located about 20m from the building, which feeds into a reedbed and then a soakaway.

Natural and Recycled Materials

Earthship Brighton obviously fully embraced the concept of using recycled materials, such as used tyres, bottles, aluminium cans and recycled timber, and natural materials, such as the earth, that is excavated to create an earthship. Various sources were also used for recycled timber and 'waste' stone, such as stone off-cut donations from the ends of stone veins in commercial quarries.

Water Harvesting

A butterfly-roof serves to collect rainwater, which is stored in four eco-vat tanks, buried near the roof level of the earthship, so that rainwater is gravity-fed to the WOM (water organizing module). Each of the storage tanks has a 5,000ltr capacity, making a total water storage limit of 20,000ltr (4,400 gallons). The cool and dark environment of underground water storage tanks discourages bacteria. Water is used and recycled until it reaches the blackwater stage, in line with the earthship approach.

Food Production

Earthship Brighton has about twice the area of internal planters as Earthship Fife, for potential food production – about 14m² (150ft²). As the building acts as a community centre for Stanmer Organics, who lease land nearby to produce organic food, it is obviously surrounded by land with great potential for self-sufficiency.

CONCLUSIONS

Earthships, which seem extraordinary at first glance, are certainly one extreme and idiosyncratic solution to the problem of designing and building the zero-carbon house. In many ways they are a return to a former more sustainable age, where all one's resources were more or less in the immediate vicinity of our habitation before the age of electricity, apart from the high-tech bits, and these are effectively the 'rocket science' part, as technologies such as photo-voltaics and water purification largely came out of the space race. Ironically, NASA-developed technology for survival in a hostile environment, such as space or another planet, is adapted for survival on our increasingly less benign environment here on earth. There is also something of the pioneering, Wild West spirit about them, appropriately enough – and it makes sense to be completely off-grid, when there is no grid for many kilometres.

However, despite the theoretical proposals for higher density concentrations of earthships, in multi-storey scenarios, it is difficult to conceive of us all living in earthships. About half of us live in cities, largely out of economic necessity, and there are economies of scale from such densities. Clearly the infrastructural grids contained within conurbations also have benefits, largely because they are already there – it is difficult to justify the entire populations of cities going off-grid and living the earthship lifestyle, unless we live in much lower densities. But will there be enough space for that anyway? Earthships are undoubtedly an ideal zero-carbon dwelling solution – for the lucky few.

CHAPTER SUMMARY

- Earthships are so-called because they are autonomous and self-contained dwellings, which provide all the necessities of life to sustain their inhabitants.
- Michael Reynolds, the maverick American architect, is their inventor and he has experimented with innovative dwellings in the desert of New Mexico for the last four decades.
- Earthships began in the 1970s near Taos, New

Mexico. They were as much about building your own house from found and waste materials to avoid mortgage payments, as experimenting with low-energy buildings.
- There is a long and venerable history of building houses from waste materials, such as bottles, particularly in the USA. Western gold-rush towns in California and Nevada frequently featured a 'bottle house' made entirely from empty booze and snake-oil remedy bottles.
- Earthships are now built in every state of the USA and most other countries around the world. They are applicable to all climatic conditions, if adapted appropriately from their New Mexican prototypes.
- The earthship concept is a way of treading lightly on the earth and approaching self-sufficiency. There are now off-the-peg earthship plan packages and components available from Solar Survival Architecture in New Mexico. They can be zero-carbon houses or celebrity lifestyle statements, such as Earthship Weaver in Colorado.
- Earthships heat and cool themselves naturally; collect their own power from the sun, wind and hydro; harvest their own water; produce their own food; and treat their own sewage on-site. The documentary film *Garbage Warrior* catalogues the tale of Michael Reynolds and earthships.
- Michael Reynolds, the maverick American architect or 'ecotect' as he likes to be called, invented and evolved the earthship concept during the energy crises of the 1970s. He refers to his approach as 'biotecture' and aims for harmony with nature and the cyclical use of the earth's resources.
- The first principle of earthship design is thermal and solar heating and cooling. The thermal mass of the massive earth berm structure of the back retaining wall, with dense earth pounded into the old tyres, is one of the key concepts of the earthship. The front of the earthship is designed to maximize winter solar gain and exclude the high-summer sun angles, which would cause overheating. In extremely hot climates, air is cooled by passing it through an earth tunnel,

where it loses heat to the cool thermal mass of the ground, before it enters the interior.

- The second principle of earthship design is the provision of reduced energy demand from renewable resources, such as the sun, wind and water, with the inclusion of a wood-burning stove to provide a comforting hearth. A 'POM' or Power Organizing Module controls the electricity supply and a battery system maintains an emergency supply to allow for the conveniences of a modern lifestyle. The first principle reduces energy demand, while the second principle needs optimal renewable energy 'system sizing' to be economical.

- The third principle of earthship design is contained sewage treatment. Water is too precious a commodity for a drop of it to be wasted. Sewage in an earthship refers to 'blackwater' from the toilet. Greywater from the sinks, shower and so on are processed into the water-recycling system. All of the solids and waste water from the WC are treated by natural processes in what are known as the 'botanical cells'. These are entirely sealed from the surrounding earth with an impervious liner to prevent seepage, and the sewage nourishes plants.

- The fourth principle of earthship design is the use of natural and recycled materials, such as used tyres, bottles and cans to create walls that are then plastered with adobe. Earthship builders who are wholly in pursuit of the junk aesthetic will re-use as many materials and components as they can to reduce the embodied energy of their building's fabric to less than zero carbon.

- The fifth principle of earthship design is water-harvesting from rain and snow melt captured on the roof, which is then filtered, purified and stored in a large cistern beneath the structure. Water is recycled in an earthship system: rainwater is harvested and purified to make it drinkable; the greywater waste is then used to water the internal planters in the conservatory; toilet flushing is the next use; and the final use is as 'blackwater' or sewage that nourishes plants that turn it back into harmless water. A WOM is used to control water consumption.

- The sixth principle of earthship design is food production. Food and flora is grown in the internal greywater planters. Most earthships need some surrounding land to approach food-production self-sufficiency. Some recent earthships have a third of their floor area given over to food production, including livestock such as fish, chickens and goats, the latter also providing for the production of eggs and cheese.

CHAPTER 6

Communities

Even if some natural event such as a series of large volcanic eruptions or a decrease of solar radiation reprieves us, it still will have been better to spend our money and our efforts making our country self-sufficient in food and energy and, if we are to become wholly urban, then making cities that we are proud to live in.

James Lovelock (2009)

ECONOMIES OF ZERO-CARBON SCALE

When the zero-carbon house is scaled up into larger multi-residential developments, or even to the scale of the town or village, clear economies of scale are produced. Zero-carbon housing developments also allow for the consideration of issues beyond the construction, maintenance and energy use of the individual house. The collective impact of the zero-carbon housing development allows a wider influence on the surrounding geographical context and infrastructure. Issues such as food production, transport networks, consumer goods and waste become far more efficient at the scale of an ecological community. At the scale of ecological communities or eco-towns, such as Vauban in Freiburg and Hammaby Sjostad near Stockholm, it becomes easier for residents to practise sustainable or even carbon-neutral lifestyles to complement their zero-carbon houses. Primarily the buildings themselves will have to be highly energy efficient or carbon neutral, using renewable energy resources, efficient infrastructure, close proximity to employment opportunities and services – such as the living and adjacent workspaces in developments such as Beddington Zero carbon Development (BedZED).

It is only by scaling up the concept of the zero-carbon house to that of the zero-carbon community, village, town or city that we have any chance of living within the sustainable resources of our one planet, rather than the current three-planet lifestyles pursued by average individuals in the UK; not to mention the five planets that would be needed to satisfy the average consumption per head in the USA. Half of the average carbon dioxide emissions of the average UK resident is comprised of the three categories of housing provision or construction, home energy use, which uses about a quarter, and transport, which uses another quarter. So these areas are good areas to prioritize in the quest for zero-carbon existence. Food and consumer goods make up nearly another quarter. The following seven categories are a convenient way of approaching systematic environmental impact reduction:

1. Construction and maintenance.
2. Energy use.
3. Transport.
4. Food.
5. Consumer goods.
6. Business services and infrastructure.
7. Waste.

ABOVE: **South-facing housing units at BedZED in south London, UK.**

BELOW: **View over roof terraces above the work units at BedZED, London, UK.**

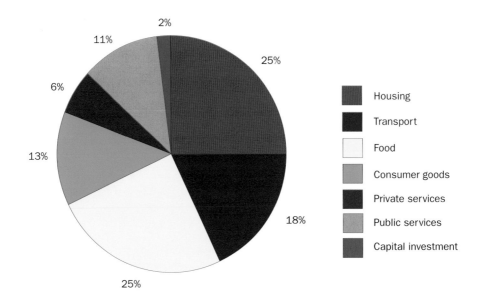

UK ecological footprint by category.

1. Construction and Maintenance

This category represents roughly 10 per cent of the average ecological footprint and a similar order of the carbon dioxide emissions of the average UK resident. In order to build zero-carbon housing, we need to use low embodied energy in the construction materials, and design and build durable buildings with an increased design life. Additionally, we must design for the eventual demolition or recycling of these materials, so that they can be re-used at the end of the building's life. Minimum domestic building lifecycles are at least sixty years, but looking around at our existing housing stock shows robust houses that are centuries old. Greater resource efficiency, such as the increased use of recycled and reclaimed materials, reducing waste during construction and reducing infrastructure, are good steps towards zero-carbon housing.

The carbon footprint of housing construction includes the impact of the construction industry, and the building operation and maintenance of our housing. Targets of zero-carbon housing are extremely challenging if they are to be met solely by using materials that have lower embodied energy. A combination of low carbon and durable materials is necessary. There must also be the ability to demolish and recycle materials, if necessary, summarized as the following priorities:

- Lower embodied energy of materials.
- Durable housing with an increased design life.
- Design for demolition, so the materials can be recycled.

Refurbishing the existing housing stock to achieve zero-carbon performance will also be necessary.

Building zero-carbon housing on a large scale also results in an economy of scale in terms of the shared infrastructure, such as roads and drainage systems, and so on. The embodied carbon dioxide of housing has a wide range but can be measured in the weight of carbon dioxide per metre square, per hundred homes. This currently ranges from best practice of 300kg to worst practice of 1,000kg of carbon dioxide per metre square, per hundred homes. Embodied carbon dioxide of infrastructure

ABOVE: **Stone-wall cottage with turf roof displays high thermal mass, CAT, Wales.**

BELOW: **CAT stone cottage temperature monitor – stable internal temperatures on a hot day.**

will often be reduced if houses are built in multiple units, as at BedZED. Savings of around 60 per cent carbon dioxide emission reductions are possible through greater resource efficiency, such as increasing the amount of recycled and reclaimed materials, reducing construction-site wastage of materials and reducing the amount of built infrastructure by shared use.

Green concrete is a good example of a recycled material, as it consists of 100 per cent recycled aggregate and 50 per cent cement replacement – this reduces the embodied carbon by a third. Although sustainable materials such as timber, which are renewable by their very nature, can be used in low- to zero-carbon construction, it is also necessary to design for thermal mass in housing. Materials, such as concrete, which have the ability to absorb heat in the summer and release it in the winter, and during colder nights, are necessary to stabilize temperatures, particularly as we approach increasing temperatures through global warming and climate change.

2. Energy Use

This category includes all gas and electricity consumption, and other fuels such as coal and gas. Eco-town and eco-village developers can help residents to reduce the impact of their domestic energy use, which usually is about a quarter of an individual's carbon dioxide emissions, by creating zero-carbon housing. Ecological housing should be energy efficient and built to Level 4 of the code for sustainable homes at the very least – Level 6 is zero carbon. Houses need to be fitted with super-efficient appliances. Eco-towns will have to operate completely on renewable energy, or as close to that as possible. At least half of this should be on-site renewable generation. Energy supply should be delivered efficiently. In terms of monitoring, live energy consumption figures should be supplied for each house to help with behaviour change.

3. Transport

Personal transport, together with the building and maintenance of roads and motorways makes up about a quarter of each person's carbon dioxide emissions. To achieve ecological sustainability targets this has to reduce by about 80 per cent. The whole aim of eco-towns, villages and housing communities is to dramatically reduce the need to travel, by placing workplaces and homes very close by and providing sustainable travel options. Community facilities and workplaces have to be within walking and cycling distances. This usually means average densities of around 50 houses per hectare, nearer to 100 houses per hectare in central, denser areas. This should allow easy walking and cycling to major local facilities. Moves away from complete reliance on cars should also have an improved effect on local communities and allow people to get to know each other again; not to mention the obvious improvements to air quality, noise pollution and so on.

Local employment opportunities should also reduce the need to travel and commute. Ideally zero-carbon communities will not use fossil fuels for either dwellings or transport. Looked at in

Energy meter readings displayed at eye level, with a vision panel door, in the kitchens at BedZED.

more detail this means that the average walking time to shops, schools, post offices and other key local facilities should not be more than ten to fifteen minutes. BedZED includes public transport within ten minutes' walk; incentives for bicycle use and storage of them inside dwellings; London's first car club; home zones and reduced car parking; a charge for car-parking spaces and a car-parking permit system. Monitoring over several years of occupation at BedZED showed that the use of private-car, fossil fuel miles travelled compared with the local average was in the order of 50 to 65 per cent lower. Only 17 per cent of BedZED residents travel to work by car, while the local average is 42 per cent.

Air travel, obviously encouraged by cheap fares, remains the perennial carbon bugbear and adds as much as a third to individual's carbon dioxide emission impacts for each long-haul flight. Our dependence on air travel was highlighted recently, when it was interrupted by the antics of a certain Icelandic volcano, which wrought chaos and stranded travellers, at first. However, further volcanic eruptions and continued uncertainty have undoubtedly brought about behavioural changes, which could well be a foretaste of a zero-carbon future. Eco-communities must also provide low-carbon public transport options. The frequency of public transport options of around ten to fifteen minutes in the daytime is normally necessary to avoid the default to car use. This must be supported by real-time displays showing public transport departure times and actual running information. Targets should be in the range of 75 per cent reduction in miles travelled by private car when compared with local averages.

Food Miles

Food miles are the distance that food travels from the farm until it ends up on your plate. Reasonable estimates are that food travels a few thousand miles every time it is delivered to your kitchen. As globalization has increased, the food miles have increased by about a quarter in the last few decades. Food miles are one way of measuring the environmental impact of food production. The longer supply lines of food, and our desire for out-of-season products flown from the other side of the world, have led to some estimates that the ingredients of a typical British Sunday lunch is nearly 50,000 miles. It is difficult to imagine such trends continuing as oil prices increase – as it would be neither economic nor sustainable.

There are many variables and problems with this simple one-dimensional measure of environmental impact. For example, the method of transport is not usually included: as ships can be much more effective than lorries or aeroplanes, this is important. Food transported on roads produces the most carbon dioxide emissions, as nearly two-thirds of the world's food is transported on the roads. However, recent studies in North America and the UK suggest that about 80 per cent of emissions are produced before the food leaves the farm gate. The calculation of excessive food miles would suggest that locally produced food is the best way to go. Studies have shown that transportation is of minor importance compared to carbon emissions from pesticide and fertilizer production, not to mention the fuel required by farming and food processing.

Critics of food miles also suggest that food should be produced by the most efficient producers, and cite the example of New Zealand lamb being shipped to the UK, asserting that to produce the same amount of lamb in Britain would use about three times the carbon dioxide emissions per tonne because of all the feed and fertilizer needed on British pastures. There is also the question of improving livelihoods in developing countries through agricultural development. Whatever your view there is certainly a feel-good factor about consuming locally produced food, not to mention growing your own food in a kitchen garden or allotment. Plucking a carrot or potato from outside your kitchen window certainly seems to make more sense than flying them thousands of miles around the world.

4. Food

Food production and processing accounts for £80 billion of the UK economy and is the largest manufacturing sector. Food consumption in the UK represents 8 per cent of our total individual CO_2 emissions, and is responsible for nearly a quarter of our individual ecological footprint – food production needs large land areas. Intensive agricultural methods are constantly highlighted in the media, by various 'TV chefs', but free-range and organic farming methods generally need even more land, but obviously with less adverse environmental impacts.

Many consumers are voting with their feet and supporting a lower carbon system by buying food with a smaller environmental footprint, which is usually locally produced. Vegetarians also had their halos polished by recent media attention on the carbon intensity of livestock production, as a sixth of our greenhouse gas emissions is due to food production, mainly the methane emissions from livestock flatulence. Methane is twenty-five times more powerful than carbon dioxide as a greenhouse gas, and estimated to be responsible for 20 per cent of man-made global warming.

5. Consumer Goods

Consumer goods means any product we purchase, from large, long-term household items, such as furniture and fridges, to more ephemeral stuff, such as clothing, publications and electronics. Consumer goods account for 14 per cent of an individual's ecological footprint and 13 per cent of CO_2 emissions in the UK. We live in a consumerist society, where economic growth is paramount – unfortunately, this also leads to a throw-away society with built-in obsolescence in most products. Clearly, there are potential contradictions between reducing the environmental impact of consumerism and economic growth. Probably, the best way for consumers to reduce such impacts is to vote with their feet and purchase green products, such as A-rated white goods and recycled products.

This was quite aptly illustrated by the recent UK Government's automobile scrappage scheme, where a £2,000 discount on the purchase of a new car was offered in exchange for trading in your old car, which had to be at least ten years old. Ten years does not seem very old for such a major purchase as a car, but I speak as someone who is driving a fifteen-year-old car with a mileage of 210,000 miles, which is still going very well due to regular servicing and maintenance. There is such a large amount of embodied energy in a vehicle that is seems sensible to maintain its life as long as possible, but there is also a point at which cleaner and more efficient technologies supersede this whole-life costing argument. Clearly, I will have to buy an electric car soon!

Recycled glass and re-used bottles become drinking glasses.

6. Infrastructure

All of us have to accept a proportion of responsibility for our country-wide carbon footprint, gen-

Electric car connected to charging post.

erated as a result of government and business services and infrastructure, including administration of central and local government, plus services that they manage, such as social services, waste management, schools and universities. This is about a quarter of an individual's ecological impact and is described as a national responsibility. It includes all infrastructure and services not included in the construction and operation of homes, energy, transport and consumer goods. Obviously, individuals have little control over this impact, apart from when taking part in a local or national political election – and the 2010 annual election saw the UK Green Party's first Member of Parliament elected in Brighton.

7. Waste

Waste rarely shows up as a category in its own right, as it is spread across all sectors. It is clearly an important and potentially easy area to tackle. Periods of economic austerity, such as war time, generally provide some good examples of lateral thinking in the use of resources, parsimony and the reduction of wasteful practices. And British Member of Parliament, Colin Challen has compared the challenge of climate change to a 'twilight war', which will shortly influence everything that we do.

There are also some extremely good examples of reducing and eliminating waste in Third World countries, where manufactured items are at a

133

Bill Dunster, Zero Hero

The British ecological architect, or eco-architect, Bill Dunster worked for the architectural firm of Michael Hopkins and Partners for about fifteen years, before he designed the Beddington Zero Energy Development (BedZED). Dunster specialized in low energy and sustainable developments while working with Hopkins. His final project at the firm was Nottingham University New Campus, for which he was project architect and took the scheme from inception to completion. The building was opened in late 1999 by Queen Elizabeth II and was awarded the Stirling Prize and the RIBA Sustainability Award. Bill has also taught at the Architectural Association and Kingston University in London. He was awarded an OBE for services to sustainable housing design in 2010.

He built his own prototype, low-energy, live-and-work concept building, called Hope House, in 1995, in which he still lives and works. Dunster still uses his own house 'like a test rig, so before we inflict our ideas on others, we're finding out what works. The house is built with all the standard things you get from builders merchants – there's nothing clever about it'. The aptly named Hope House, and an earlier student project at Edinburgh University for a housing estate fuelled by solar power (his teachers thought he was nuts, apparently), provided the test bed for the scaled-up zero energy community that became the seminal BedZED.

In 1999 Bill Dunster designed BedZED for the Peabody Trust, which was built on the site of a former water-treatment works in South London. BedZED is an environmentally friendly energy-efficient mix of housing and workspace, which has won a range of awards, including the RIBA Sustainability Award. BedZED was also short-listed for the Stirling Prize. Bill's guiding philosophy, and the imperative he recognized several years ago – that we must build zero carbon buildings now – has become enshrined in his architectural practice's philosophy. Bill Dunster Associates and Zedfactory Ltd start from the standpoint of the question, how can we reduce our environmental impact whilst increasing our quality of life?

Dunster estimates that the UK population's average lifestyle is using three planets: one third, or one planet, for heating and powering homes; another third for the food miles from farm to plate (the UK imports 70 per cent of its food); and the final third coming from transport car use and commuting. The first priority is reducing demand and to reduce the amount of energy that buildings use. Further responses include designing out the need for travel and commuting by locating residential and workspaces cheek-by-jowl. And future-proofing

Bill Dunster – sustainable housing pioneer.

BedZED – detail of the south façade apartments.

communities by designing long life, loose fit, low-energy building shells or envelopes, capable of being changed from residential to commercial use and back again, if necessary. Additionally, food should be produced locally.

Tactically, to reduce the amount of energy buildings use, we should begin with the reduction of electrical loads and specify low-energy appliances and not using electric water-heating. Using natural ventilation and high levels of natural daylight can reduce electrical use by about a quarter. Second, we need to reduce the space-heating loads to near zero, by the use of super-insulated building envelopes. Third, thermal mass is created by exposed heavyweight construction, such as concrete or masonry, and reduces heating and cooling load by storage of thermal energy. Finally, airtight construction drastically reduces winter heat loss through infiltration or unwanted ventilation. Ventilating through wind cowls with heat-recovery reduces excess heat-loss and maintains good air quality.

The final strand of the ZED philosophy maintains that once energy demand is significantly reduced, it should be possible for the building to supply its own energy from renewable sources, for example, a split between electrical generation from photovoltaic solar panels and micro-wind turbines. Thermal generation is through passive solar gain, such as south-facing sun spaces, to reduce heating loads and evacuated solar collectors. Finally, biomass boilers, using carbon neutral wood pellets, satisfy what little heating demand that remains in winter.

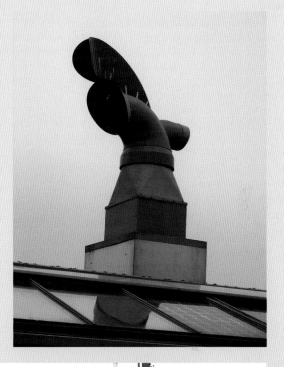

TOP: **Wind cowl on the roof of the BedZED development.**

BOTTOM: **Biomass energy centre at BedZED.**

premium – 'waste' collection of items, such as cardboard, is a cottage industry in India. The extraordinary case study of the city of Curitiba, in southern Brazil, has also turned 'waste' into an important industry, with the slogan of 'waste that is not waste' for its recycling programme.

The avoidance of waste, as far as possible, is an obvious starting point, after which unavoidable waste has to be construed as a resource to be reprocessed into something useful, or processed to recover value or energy from it. Domestic recycling has to be made easy for residents with a zero-carbon target of no waste going to landfill. The media in the UK recently made much of the shocking statistics that Britons waste about a third of their food. Some organic waste is inevitable, but treating this on-site by composting is one solution. Zero-carbon developers will need to work with local authorities, retailers and businesses to reduce waste. Waste minimization strategies to reduce waste arising by between 25 per cent and 50 per cent are a start.

A CONVENIENT TRUTH

Urban Solutions from Curitiba, Brazil

Curitiba is the largest city in southern Brazil and also the largest economy in that area. It is the seventh largest city in Brazil with a total population of about 3 million. The name derives from the indigenous dialect and means 'much pine', a description of the surrounding countryside that still holds true. Historically, the city was an important cattle-trading centre, located between the coast and the cattle breeding hinterland. The area was first encountered by Europeans in 1530, and was little more than a collection of gold-mining encampments

Location of Curitiba in Southern Brazil.

throughout most of the seventeenth century. The bulk of European immigration took place in the mid-nineteenth century, mainly from Germany, Italy, Poland and the Ukraine, spurred by political upheavals in Europe and the attraction of the temperate climate in Curitiba. The European influx created new industries, such as agriculture, forestry and wood-working. Nowadays, the city is an important cultural, political and economic centre, which is the capital of the large province of Paraná.

The lessons that the rest of the world can learn from Curitiba originated in the 1970s, when the city took a radical and visionary path of sustainable economic development, at odds with events that were taking place in the rest of Brazil, not to mention most of the rest of the world. Most of the rest of Brazil welcomed inward industrial development in the 1970s, regardless of the potential environmental and social side-effects of polluting industries. This was a path that Curitiba chose not to take, instead they insisted on accepting only non-polluting industries and built an industrial district with so much green space that it was derided as a 'golf-course' by competing conurbations.

This cynicism evaporated rapidly as Curitiba filled up with major businesses and overtook most of its competing cities in Latin America. The production of green space is the first of five strategies that were key to Curitiba's success, along with: the 'structural axes' (corridors of development to avoid urban sprawl); public transport system; attracting foreign investment; and 'incremental projects' (modest, pragmatic projects that give quick feedback, rather than grandiose plans). Curitiba's economic growth rate over the last three decades is several percentage points higher than the Brazilian national average of about 4 per cent, and per capita income is 66 per cent higher than the Brazilian average.

The success of Curitiba as an eco-city is based on the triple bottom line of environmental, economic and social sustainability. This story was celebrated in an hour-long documentary film called *A Convenient Truth: Open Solutions from Curitiba, Brazil*, by filmmaker Maria Vaz in 2006. However, some argue that much of the 'miracle' of Curitiba was made possible by a centralization of planning

power, not possible in democracies, created by the military dictatorship that held sway in Brazil from the mid-1960s to the mid-1980s. If true, this may suggest even wider, political, lessons for the 'free world', at a time when it has become fashionable to re-open the 'climate change debate' rather than take action, as aptly illustrated by the results of the Copenhagen climate change summit at the end of 2009. What is undeniable is that the brand of autocratic paternalism employed is effective in this context, and was opened to more democratic processes in recent decades.

Tellingly, most of the strategic decisions in Curitiba's sustainable development revolution were not the result of complicated optimization calculations, or endless scientific analysis, which can often produce 'paralysis by analysis' or 'information overload', but employed judgemental heuristics, more commonly known as 'rules of thumb'. As pioneers in sustainable development, the decision-makers had to make a start somewhere and learn as they went along – the most important thing was to make a start. This incrementalism was dictated by economics anyway, as there were no large budgets for grand schemes – modest ideas were implemented, which usually gave quick positive feedback to build on. This organic development sat well with the architectural problem-solving skills of most of the creators. Above all it forced a pragmatic approach, and the fact that so many other major cities around the globe are now implementing these ideas, decades later, bears testament to their legacy.

Masterplanning

Jaime Lerner, architect and three-time mayor of Curitiba, provides a convenient figurehead as the genius behind the success of the eco-city, and this seems thoroughly deserved. However, there is no doubt that he benefited from the legacy that he inherited from two previous mayors: Ney Braga and Ivo Arzua. Not to mention masterplans for Curitiba dating back to the 1960s, which emphasized public transport and pedestrianization – in stark contrast to the modernist vehicular agenda pursued at the new capital of Brazil, Brasilia. Braga was mayor from 1954 to 1958 and arranged for the military to appoint Lerner as mayor for his first term from 1971 to 1974 and a further term from 1979 to 1983, before he was elected by popular vote for his third term from 1989 to 1992.

Central authority allowed radical interventions, such as shutting down the heavily congested, main commercial street, and transforming it with the help of armed police into a pedestrianized area in the space of seventy-two hours, over a weekend, before anyone could complain too much. This was done with the proviso that, if the retailers were not happy about the intervention in six months, it would be returned to its former situation.

Unfortunately, the newly created vehicle-free precinct was quickly colonized by vagrants, but they were equally rapidly employed to keep the area clean by the administration, rather than moved on by the police, a good example of the lateral thinking that pervades the Curitiban solution. The street was shortly renamed Rua das Flores – the Street of Flowers.

Lerner contends that within a matter of weeks, retailers in nearby vehicular thoroughfares were begging for their streets to be pedestrianized, when the experience of the first intervention showed dramatically increased trade. Pedestrians were able

Jaime Lerner, Eco-Hero

Jaime Lerner, the three-time mayor of Curitiba and twice governor of the State of Paraná, was born in 1937 and graduated as an architect and urban planner from the University of Paraná in 1964. Despite his technical training, it would obviously have been impossible for him to lead such transformational change without political power. Architects are quite prevalent in political careers in Brazil, partly because they are favoured over lawyers, who are allegedly perceived as corrupt. In the mid-1960s he helped create the Institute of Urban Planning and Research of Curitiba and participated in the drafting of the Curitiba Master Plan (Guidlelines) published in the late 1960s.

In his first term as mayor, in the early 1970s, he set about the sustainable redevelopment of the city, assisted by a hand-picked team of technocrats. These included increasing the amount of green space to 50 square metres per inhabitant, from only several, which also allowed natural flood control of the River Iguacu. Additionally, he instigated the Bus Rapid Transit system and a host of other social, ecological and urban reforms, employing unorthodox solutions to Curitiba's geographical challenges.

He used his time as governor of the southern Brazilian province to attract investments of over US$20 billion between 1995 and 2001. This turned Paraná into one of Brazil's industrial hubs, but in an ecologically sensitive fashion. Lerner was awarded the UNICEF Child and Peace prize in 1996 for several of his programmes. He is past president of the Inter-

national Union of Architects (UIA), a professor at the Federal University of Paraná and a guest professor at the University of California Berkeley.

I was lucky enough to attend a post-screening interview with Jaime Lerner, after the Curitiba documentary, at the British Film Institute. His response to the somewhat

Jaime Lerner – sustainable development pioneer.

propaganda style of the film was to describe his city as 'not a paradise', but suffering from the same problems as every other city. The nature of the response is where the difference lies. Equally charismatically, he responded to the praise of an obviously overwhelmed member of the audience, who described him as an angel or a saint, by saying that he would prefer the 'vouchers' while he was here on earth – it struck me as pragmatic analogy of the Curitiban 'single-fare' ticket system!

Lerner frequently contends that 'cities are not as complicated as the merchants of complexity would have us believe' and that the example of Curitiba can be followed anywhere, even in New York City. He asserts that the starting point is 'a team of idealistic, fantastic people. Second is the simplicity of our approach', and that 'I believe that the major achievement of the municipal authorities is the suitable selection of technology which adequately meets the city's needs'.

Venice – a compact and car-free city.

to stop and shop rather than whizzing through in a car. The philosophy of cities being for people rather than vehicles was continued – vehicles would have their place, but they would not dominate the spaces for people. Through traffic was limited to five major highways, as part of the masterplan, along which commercial growth was encouraged. Public transport, in the form of a colour-coded bus system was at the heart of the drive to make transport more efficient and sustainable. This reduces rush-hour congestion, as well as centralizing commercial and retail activity activities, to make the suburbs more viable with local shops and businesses integrated into housing policies.

Transportation
Curitiba has a long history of public transport, with

trolley buses pulled by mules introduced in the late-nineteenth century, replaced by electric trams in 1912, in turn replaced with buses in the late-1920s. This system became outdated for Curitiba's growing needs and was replaced with the Bus Rapid Transport (BRT) in the mid-1970s, with its three-lane system with dedicated bus lanes and one-way travel system. The buses are colour-coded for express long distance (Speedy Bus), medium and short distance travel. A one-fare system was introduced, so that longer distance travel to and from the suburbs (with lower-income residents) was subsidized by shorter distance travellers in the city centre. The system is self-financing and run by the private sector, who are paid on a passenger-mile basis as an incentive.

It is estimated that around 80 per cent of the

population use the bus system, which has stops every half-kilometre in the city centre. Popular, reliable and convenient public transport is the solution to reducing traffic congestion, reducing pollution and improving air quality in city centres. Additionally, alternative renewable fuels are cheaper and less polluting. Similar systems have now been partially adopted in many other cities around the world including Los Angeles, Seattle and New York. Latterly, Curitiba has investigated other public transport systems, such as subways, but they are estimated as up to a hundred times more expensive as a bus system. In terms of social and economic sustainability this means that Curitibans spend about a tenth of their income on travel, which is far below the Brazilian national average.

Housing

One of the main social sustainability aspects of Curitiba is the social-housing model, which aims to develop affordable housing, integrated with local businesses and shopping to avoid the usual monotonous social-housing model and the creation of isolated ghettos. Sustainable public-housing solutions were an imperative due to the rapidly expanding population of the city, caused by

Colour-coded domestic recycling bins at BedZED.

unskilled rural immigration from the surrounding countryside. Home businesses, with commercial premises on the ground floor, from furniture making to ice-cream parlours, were part of the vision, so that citizens could live above the shop and receive training in their chosen skills; this was one example of the series of projects. Viable and fully integrated suburbs also relieve pressures on the city centre, and obviate commuting. Rural initiatives to help people stay in rural areas outside the city were also pursued in order to reduce the massive population growth.

Recycling

Curitiba was given a United Nations award in 1994 for its innovative approach to rubbish collection, separation and recycling – the approach began in the 1970s. The influx of unskilled workers from the hinterland of Curitiba means that the city has not eliminated favelas or shanty towns on its urban margins. However, a series of enlightened initiatives helps to alleviate some of the associated social and economic problems. One of these was the 'Trash that is not trash' scheme, which involved employing favela dwellers to collect rubbish from their shanty towns (inaccessible for large rubbish-collection vehicles anyway) and trade it for bus passes and food. As well as improving sanitary conditions in the favelas, this approach provided the raw materials for a recycling station to maximize the value of recycling in imaginative ways. This campaign was also successfully extended to the entire city. The recycling station also employs the socially marginalized, such as the homeless, while running education programmes so they can improve themselves to secure better jobs. The programme improves sanitation, reduces landfill and provides an income for rubbish collectors. Domestic recycling has to be made easy for residents.

Parks

The increasingly global problem of controlling floods from watercourses due to dramatic climate change and heavy downpours of rainfall found yet another simple solution in Curitiba. The central idea was that the traditional civil-engineering solution, of creating concrete canals to channel flood waters, just takes the problem downstream, and risks breached flood defences. Instead, linear parks were designed around the natural flows of rivers, which changed floodplains from problems into parks that provide recreational facilities and wildlife, while the lakes created emergency reservoirs for flood waters. The international recommendations for the area of green space per inhabitant in cities is 12 square metres – Curitibans have 50 square metres. Additionally, land values around the new parks were increased, which improves the economics for sustainable development. A typical example of the lateral thinking involved is the importation of flocks of sheep to the parks, to provide natural maintenance and grass cutting!

Final Words from Jaime Lerner

The environmentally correct city should give preeminence to collective over individual transport, economizing fuel and reducing the need for investments in various public works. The environmentally correct city avoids forced industrialization, rejects polluting industries, and obliges government and producers to invest in clean technology. The environmentally correct city intervenes to avoid the segregation of urban functions and social classes. The integration of urban functions helps the city to economize or maximize because it reduces the number of dislocations. Just as the city ought to be environmentally correct, so too, it should become socially correct.

The first step is to invest in children, opening the paths of equality to those who are most in need, and in so doing, reducing the impact of poverty. A socially correct city should invest to the maximum in works that deal with the quality of life, in order to improve the city and create employment. It should optimize collective transport, which, in addition to reducing the number of automobiles in the streets, democratizes the access to urban acoutrements. The socially correct city should democratize leisure, increasing the extent of green areas, parks, bicycle paths, and all of the meeting places of its inhabitants.

CASE STUDIES

Case Study: Beddington Zero Energy Development (BedZED), London

Key Points – Project Objectives

- No use of fossil fuels.
- 50 per cent reduction of the energy used for transport.
- 60 per cent reduction in domestic energy, compared to average British households.
- 90 per cent reduction of heating needs.
- Use of renewable energy.
- 30 per cent reduction in water consumption.
- Reduce waste and encourage recycling.
- Use construction materials from local providers within a 60km radius.
- Development of local resources, such as a farmers' network for local food.
- Develop biodiversity in the natural areas.

General

The Beddington Zero Energy Development, or BedZED, is the UK's largest and most ambitious mixed-use sustainable community. It was developed by the Peabody Trust, a long-standing social housing provider, but is essentially the brainchild of the architect Bill Dunster. BedZED was designed in the late-1990s and completed in 2002, but it is the result of a considerable design evolution on the part of the architect and engineers over many years. The Peabody Trust is one of the largest social housing associations in London, and is long-established with a history spanning 150 years; it currently manages about 20,000 homes. The architect's primary concerns were fully harnessing renewable natural resources, achieving rational materials use, site-resource autonomy, social involvement, and how all of these could respond to ever-increasing lifestyle expectations.

BedZED is the UK's first and largest carbon neutral eco-community and is located in the south London borough of Sutton, a residential town about half-an-hour's train journey from central London. BedZED consists of 82 residential homes with a mixture of tenures: about half are privately-owned; a quarter are in key-worker shared-ownership; and the remaining quarter are rented social housing. The development also contains 1,600m^2 of workspace, an on-site shop, café, sports facilities; health centre and childcare facilities. The first residents moved into BedZED in March 2002 and there are 220 people currently in residence, several years later. The ambitious target was to create a net-zero, fossil-energy development, which will produce at least as much energy from renewable sources as it consumes.

The holistic and highly ambitious objectives of BedZED did come at a price – development costs turned out to be 30 per cent higher than first anticipated. The price of a BedZED home is about 20 per cent higher than the average price of an apartment in the same area. However, it should also be remembered that you are buying into the lifestyle and the means to live more sustainably and economically. The construction of BedZED is not that far away from some of the concepts of earthships, as BedZED is made from the thermally-massive materials, such as concrete blocks and concrete slabs, which store heat during warm conditions and release heat at cooler times.

The houses are arranged in south-facing terraces to maximize solar gain and there are several hundred square metres of photovoltaic solar panels, mainly on the south-facing façades. The work units and office are located on the north side of the blocks, where minimal solar gain reduces overheating and avoids the need for air conditioning. The homes are fitted with low-energy lighting and energy-efficient appliances to reduce electrical requirements.

There is also a small-scale combined heat and power (CHP) unit, which is fuelled by sustainably

BedZED south-facing housing units, London, UK.

Case Study: Beddington Zero Energy Development (BedZED), London *(continued)*

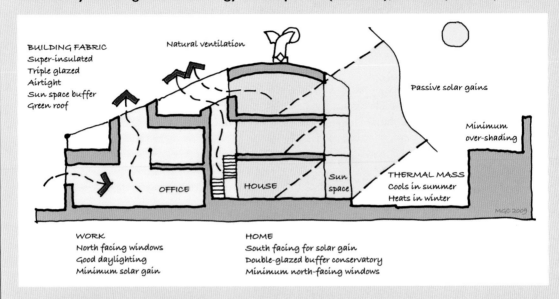

BUILDING FABRIC
Super-insulated
Triple glazed
Airtight
Sun space buffer
Green roof

Natural ventilation

Passive solar gains

Minimum
over-shading

OFFICE   HOUSE   Sun space

THERMAL MASS
Cools in summer
Heats in winter

MGC 2009

WORK
North facing windows
Good daylighting
Minimum solar gain

HOME
South facing for solar gain
Double-glazed buffer conservatory
Minimum north-facing windows

ABOVE: **BedZED passive energy systems.**

BELOW: **BedZED active energy systems.**

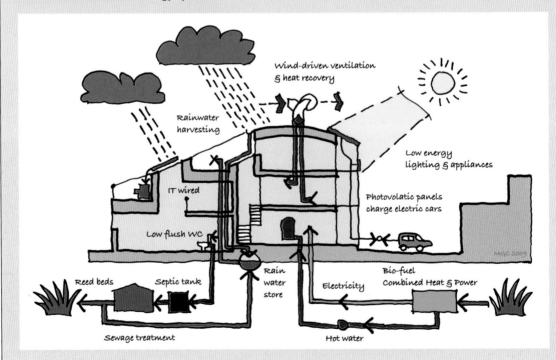

Wind-driven ventilation
& heat recovery

Rainwater
harvesting

Low energy
lighting & appliances

IT wired

Photovolatic panels
charge electric cars

Low flush WC

Reed beds   Septic tank   Rain water store   Electricity   Bio-fuel Combined Heat & Power

MGC 2009

Sewage treatment   Hot water

sourced biomass woodchips from local coppic-ing. Water use is reduced to about half of the daily use per person in the UK, to around 76ltr as opposed to around 150ltr. Recycled rainwater makes up about 20 per cent of this reduced consumption. Water-conservation features include aerated taps, low-flush WCs and smaller bath-tubs. There is a reed or water filtration system on the site, which purifies blackwater into grey-water, which can be used for toilet flushing and watering gardens.

BedZED is generally built from natural, recy-cled or reclaimed materials, and there was an emphasis on using low embodied energy material from local sources. The holistic nature of the community is intended to address the triple bot-tom line of sustainability: environmental, eco-nomic and social. The social aspects include the fact that half of the dwellings are allocated to low-income families. The overall ambition of the project was to reduce the environmental foot-print of a BedZED resident to one planet rather than the average of three planets of most British households. After several years of monitoring, 'model' residents have shown that it is possible to live within the one-planet footprint, usually by working on the site and avoiding extensive travelling, such as long-haul flights. In reality, the average lifestyle of the residents approaches two planets.

Living room and sunspace of the show flat at BedZED.

Case Study: Hockerton Housing Project, Nottingham

Key Points – Objectives

- To develop a holistic, non-polluting way of living and to work in harmony with nature – a dynamic process.
- Promote sustainable living to a wide audience.
- Promote the renewable production and efficient use of domestic energy.
- Promote affordable, ultra-low energy dwellings.
- Demonstrate that ordinary families and individuals can take responsibility for and reduce greenhouse gases that create global warming.

General

The Hockerton Housing Project is a self-build cooperative, with no space heating, and water self-sufficiency that uses less than a quarter of the energy of conventional houses. The Project was the UK's first earth-covered, self-sufficient housing development, designed by the eco-architects Brenda and Robert Vale, and built mainly by the occupants. The vision was to act as a catalyst for change and show by practical example how we can move towards ecological sound and sustainable ways of living. The Project is located near the village of Hockerton, near Nottingham, on a 10-hectare site.

The large site contains sufficient area for food production and rearing small animals, such as sheep, goats and chickens. Food production is shared by all the occupants of the terrace of five houses, using a rota system. Hockerton is now a decade old but began during the early 1990s, when, after several years of negotiating with the local council, planning permission was finally gained. The original occupants and self-builders first moved into the houses in 1998, after two years of construction work. However, all the hard works seems to have paid off, as the units are now valued at roughly quadruple the original building costs – but only a few of the houses have changed hands to newcomers buying into the lifestyle.

The houses are each about 6 metres deep with around 20 metres of south-facing conservatory frontage overlooking the lake, which also contains

Hockerton Housing Project – view over the lake to the south elevation.

Hockerton Housing Project – site plan.

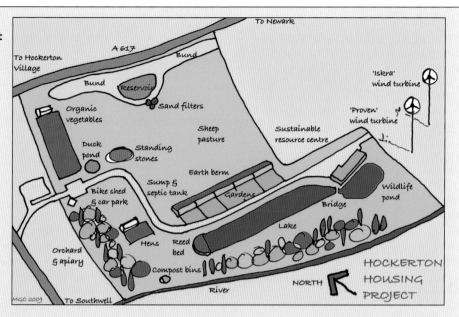

a reed bed at one end for organic sewage treatment. The dwellings are earth-sheltered with an earth berm covering the north-facing frontage. The section of the houses is designed to maximize light penetration, with the winter sun reaching the rooms at the rear. The high-angled summer sun is largely excluded from the deeper recesses of the house, which remain cool due to the high thermal mass of the concrete and earth construction, which absorbs excess heat. This stored heat is released during colder periods, such as cold nights, to stabilize internal temperatures.

Residents claim that living at Hockerton has made them more naturally in tune with nature: 'We have to be aware of the weather, the wind brings us electricity from our wind turbines, the sun brings us solar energy, and we are dependent on the rain for water supply'. Even the bricks used in the construction were fired using waste methane gas from landfill sites. In terms of food production, they inherited a small flock of sheep and now produce their own organic lamb. They also keep chickens and ducks and a small dairy cow for dairy products, as well as some beekeeping and a small amount of fish farming in the lake.

Hockerton Housing Project – interior of the conservatories.

Case Study: Hockerton Housing Project, Nottingham *(continued)*

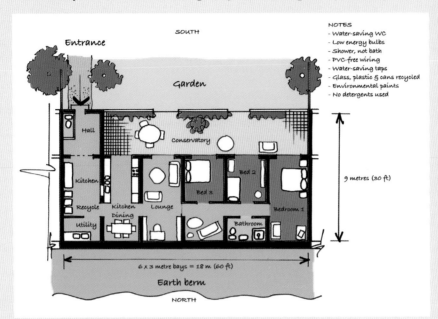

Hockerton Housing Project – house plan.

BELOW: **Hockerton Housing Project – cross-section.**

The fabric of the terrace houses is 300mm-thick concrete, with 300mm insulation, covered with 400mm of earth. This high level of thermal mass and insulation provides a stable internal temperature all year round. Rainwater falling on the conservatory roofs is collected and filtered for drinking. Water for washing and laundry is stored in a reservoir to the north of the site. Sewage is treated by reed beds at one end of the lake. There are renewable sources of energy, all year round, provided by the photovoltaic panels on the roof in summer, and the two 5kW wind-turbines on 25m-high masts in the winter.

The high-performance specification of the building fabric includes windows that are triple-glazed with low emissivity coatings, and the conservatories are double-glazed, all of which means that there is no need for a supplementary heating system. Monitoring of the internal temperatures showed them to be very stable with an

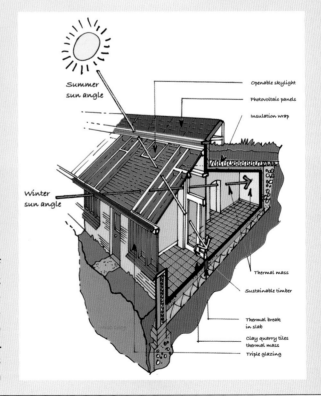

average of around 17°C during the winter, and typical summer temperatures rising to around 24°C. The temperature in the conservatory, when unshaded, regularly rose to over 30°C on sunny days. Residents report the houses are completely free of draughts and that they did not feel cold during the winter, although there was the occasional use of an electric heater on the coldest days. Some occupants also said that the houses were too warm at night, as they did not cool down like ordinary houses.

The houses were built at similar costs to traditional houses, albeit self-built, and many features could be used in mass housing developments. These include: high levels of insulation and air-tightness; the use of thermal mass to give stable internal year-round temperatures; photovoltaics; and wind turbines. The early problems experienced with the heat pumps, of damp and humidity, were resolved after the mechanical ventilation systems were used as intended, and comfort levels improved.

TOP LEFT: **Hockerton Housing Project – wind turbines.**

TOP RIGHT: **Hockerton Housing Project – south-facing conservatories.**

BOTTOM RIGHT: **Hockerton Housing Project – photovoltaic panels on the roof.**

CHAPTER SUMMARY

- When the zero-carbon house is multiplied to the urban scale, clear economies of scale are produced. The collective impact of the zero-carbon housing development allows a wider influence on the surrounding geographical context and infrastructure. Issues such as food production, transport networks, consumer goods and waste become far more efficient at the scale of an ecological community.

- Eco-urbanism is the only chance we have of living within the sustainable resources of our one-planet, rather than the current three-planet, lifestyle pursued by average individuals in the UK; or five-planet lifestyles in the USA. The following seven categories are a convenient way of approaching systematic environmental impact reduction: construction and maintenance; energy use; transport; food; consumer goods; business services and infrastructure; and waste.

- Construction and maintenance represents roughly 10 per cent of the average ecological footprint of the average UK resident. In order to build zero-carbon housing we need to use low embodied energy in the construction materials, and design and build durable buildings with an increased design life.

- Energy includes all gas and electricity consumption, and other fuels such as coal, which is usually about a quarter of an individual's carbon dioxide emissions in the UK.

- Personal transport, together with the building and maintenance of roads and motorways, makes up about a quarter of each person's carbon dioxide emissions. The whole aim of eco-towns, villages and housing communities is to dramatically reduce the need to travel, by placing workplaces and homes very close by and providing sustainable travel options.

- Food consumption in the UK represents 8 per cent of our total individual CO_2 emissions, and is responsible for nearly a quarter of our individual ecological footprint – food production needs large land areas.

- Consumer goods account for 14 per cent of an individual's ecological footprint and 13 per cent of CO_2 emissions in the UK. Probably, the best way for consumers to reduce such impacts is to vote with their feet and purchase green products, such as A-rated white goods and recycled products.

- Government and business services and infrastructure is about a quarter of an individual's ecological impact in the UK. Individuals have little control over this impact, apart from when taking part in a local or national political election.

- Curitiba is the largest city in southern Brazil, with a total population of about 3 million. The lessons that the rest of the world can learn from Curitiba originated in the 1970s, when the city took a radical and visionary path of sustainable economic development.

- The production of green space is the first of five strategies that were key to Curitiba's success, along with: the 'structural axes' (corridors of development to avoid urban sprawl); public transport system; attracting foreign investment; and 'incremental projects' (modest, pragmatic projects that give quick feedback, rather than grandiose plans).

- The success of Curitiba as an eco-city is based on the triple bottom line of environmental, economic and social sustainability. This story was celebrated in an hour-long documentary film called *A Convenient Truth: Open Solutions from Curitiba, Brazil*, by filmmaker Maria Vaz in 2006.

- The strategic decisions in Curitiba's sustainable-development revolution were arrived at by judgemental heuristics, more commonly known as 'rules of thumb'. This incrementalism was dictated by economics – modest ideas were implemented that usually gave quick positive feedback to build on. A pragmatic approach of building on small successes built up over the decades into a strategic framework of sustainable development.

- Curitiba started with the philosophy of cities being for people rather than vehicles – they would not dominate the spaces for people. Through traffic was limited to five major highways, as part of the masterplan, along which commercial growth was encouraged. Public transport, in the form of a colour-coded bus system, was at the heart of the drive to make transport more efficient and sustainable. This reduces rush-hour congestion, as well as centralizing commercial and retail activities, to make the suburbs more viable with local shops and businesses integrated into housing policies.

- 80 per cent of Curitibans use the bus system, which has stops every half-kilometre in the city centre. Similar systems have now been partially adopted in many other cities around the world including Los Angeles, Seattle and New York.
- Housing is one of the main social sustainability aspects of Curitiba. The social housing model is integrated with local businesses and shopping. Viable and fully integrated suburbs relieve pressures on the city centre, and obviate commuting.

- Recycling is a constant theme in Curitiba. A typical initiative was the 'Trash that is not trash' scheme, which involved employing favela dwellers to collect rubbish from their shanty towns (inaccessible for large rubbish collection vehicles anyway) and trade it for bus passes and food. This campaign was also successfully extended to the entire city.
- Curitiba uses linear parks, green space and lakes to alleviate flooding problems. The international recommendations for the area of green space per inhabitant in cities in 12 square metres – Curitibans have 50 square metres. Additionally, land values around the new parks are increased, which improves the economics for sustainable development. A typical example of the lateral thinking involved is the importation of flocks of sheep to the parks, to provide natural maintenance and grass cutting!

CHAPTER 7

Lifestyles

Let's face it. Our world is in deep, deep trouble and we are the troublemakers. We have to make real, difficult changes yesterday. Despite the obvious benefits, we are not going to recycle, compost or talk our way out of this ... it's up to me and you to make the choice of becoming responsible stewards of this earth. Join us on the journey towards a sustainable present and future. Let's walk the path to freedom!

Jules Dervaes (2005)

CARBON FOOTPRINTS

The quantification of what your lifestyle emits each year in carbon dioxide is something of a moot point and will depend on many different variables, not least of which are your relative affluence and geographical location. In Europe we generally average three-planet lifestyles, while in North America it is more like five planets. Clearly, as we only have one planet it would help if we tried to live one-planet lifestyles. Quite what these lifestyles equate to in terms of carbon dioxide emissions will depend on your specific behaviour and habits, but it is probably from 10 to 15 tonnes annually for the average UK resident. The Centre for Alternative Technology in Wales recommends a 2.5 tonne carbon footprint as an aspiration for sustainable living, which is based on the amount of CO_2 the planet can reabsorb and dividing it equally between each of several billion people on the planet.

Assessing Your Carbon Footprint

As the old adage goes – how do you get there? It depends on where you are starting from, as always. There are a number of websites that purport to help you calculate your carbon footprint, and they

will all do it in different ways. In the United Kingdom, you could do worse than logging on to the Energy Saving Trust's website to use their 'Carbon Cutter' application. The EST also has a free home-energy report service on the same site, which allows you to delve into more detail on your home energy use, its associated carbon impact, and gain an idea of the energy efficiency rating of your home in terms of the A to G rating on an Energy Performance Certificate.

The Carbon Cutter approach covers the three categories of: Home, Appliances and Travel. You are probably doing well if you are coming in at under 10 tonnes annually for your individual impacts on the EST's Carbon Cutter, and that will probably mean that you have not taken a long-haul flight for a while (and they let you off business travel, as it is usually beyond your control). The Carbon Cutter takes a necessarily broad approach as required by the completion of a five-minute questionnaire. It does ask you if you throw food away often, but not if you are a vegetarian. Methane from livestock is about twenty-five times as powerful as carbon dioxide in its impact as a greenhouse gas, but we are trying to assess carbon footprints.

Air travel is another tricky category for carbon calculators, and most of them probably do not take the increased impact of high-altitude carbon dioxide emissions into account. Carbon dioxide emissions at high altitude caused by aeroplane travel will have from two to two-and-a-half times (some experts claim four times!) the impact of carbon dioxide emissions on the ground – air travel is not good for your carbon footprint, or the planet. Frequent flyers will find that their habit makes up the largest part of their carbon footprint – let the train take the strain instead! CAT's estimate of the average carbon footprint of 8 tonnes generously assumes that you have managed to wean yourself off air travel.

Reducing Your Carbon Footprint

Fortunately, there are a few easy steps to shave a few tonnes of carbon equivalent off your lifestyle, simply by making some adjustments to your behaviour and undertaking a few long-overdue home improvements. Installing some loft insulation is a

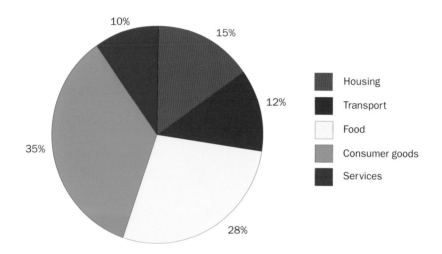

Average UK resident's annual carbon footprint.

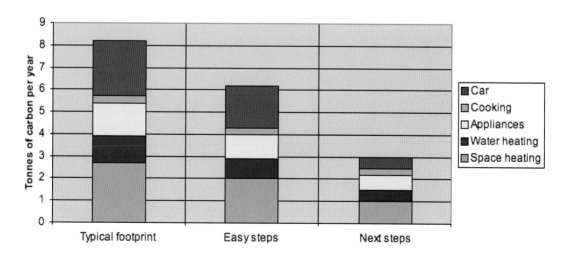

Reducing annual carbon footprints.

good starting point — topping up 100mm to 250mm should decrease your carbon footprint by at least half-a-tonne a year. Other energy-efficiency measures in your home, such as turning down the thermostat by a degree or two Centigrade and installing energy-efficient lightbulbs should save another half-tonne. Electricity has at least two to two-and-a-half times the impact of gas heating in terms of carbon dioxide emissions — turning off appliances rather than leaving them on stand-by helps. Maintain your car, invest in one with a smaller engine and walk short journeys (it's healthier!) to get your footprint down to an average of 6 tonnes, easily.

More radical steps are necessary to reduce your carbon footprint to 3 or 4 tonnes of carbon a year, such as further home-improvements like solar water-heating or a condensing boiler. Travel is another key area, with steps such as using public transport more, joining a car club, or considering alternative fuel types (e.g. biofuels). Lifestyle choices are something even individuals living in

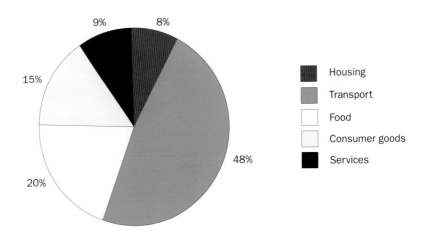

Steve's three-planet lifestyle at BedZED.

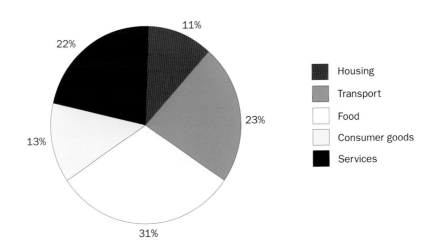

Nicole's one-planet lifestyle at BedZED.

zero-carbon housing, such as the Beddington Zero-Energy Development (BedZED) have to work at. This is typified by the contrast between two residents, Steve and Nicole. The latter has managed to live almost within the ideal one-planet lifestyle, while the former is nearer to three planets. While both live energy efficiently, it is Steve's long-haul flight holiday to the USA that has inflated his carbon footprint.

Ecological footprints are another way of examining our impact on the planet. They show the area of land that is used for our lifestyles and everything we consume. The number of planets we would need for our lifestyle is one way of expressing this – with the target of becoming a one-planet person.

In terms of land area, 1.9 hectares is an individual's fair share of the planet – the average ecological footprint in the UK is nearer to 5.5 global hectares.

TRAVEL

Cheap air-flights have become the bane of our attempts to live sustainably, and more and more of us are falling into the habit of using air travel, even for domestic and short-haul journeys. Flying has a high environmental impact and carbon-offsetting air travel is less than ideal, as it rarely includes the increased impact of carbon dioxide emissions at high altitude. Most flights are responsible for about

Typical municipal allotment in the UK.

Lucy and Molly working their allotment.

0.17kg of CO_2 per passenger-kilometre (multiplied by at least two to account for the impact of carbon emissions at high altitude). A return flight from London to continental Europe of about 2,500km emits around 1 tonne of carbon equivalent, while a long-haul, intercontinental return flight of 10,000km emits over 4 tonnes of carbon equivalent. The train is generally a fifth of the carbon impact of flying.

FOOD

Growing our own food is increasing in popularity, and comparison with the wartime efforts of Victory gardens or digging for victory is apt as we continue to do battle with global warming and climate change. A one-acre small-holding is described in John Seymour's classic book of the 1970s, *The Complete Book of Self-Sufficiency*, with a blueprint of a 5-acre holding to allow for more livestock and capable of supplying enough food for a family of four to six people. However, few of us are in possession of the perfect small-holding, let alone the time to work it, unless you take the radical step of turning your surburban plot into a micro-farm, reminiscent of the TV series *The Good Life*.

In the UK, municipal allotments are making a resurgence, and acquiring one may involve putting your name down on a waiting list – they provide a compelling introduction to home-grown vegetables and are educational for children. Most allotments are rented for around £50 a year for a 250m² plot, which is capable of producing nearly a tonne of food annually – £2,000 worth. Crop rotation is an essential art to practise, as there are several family groups of vegetables and growing the same type continuously in the same location stores up pest and disease problems. A four-year cycle is generally optimal.

Hollywood and Vines

An allotment is one thing, but in California they rarely do things by halves, as demonstrated by the Dervaes family who turned their suburban plot in Pasedena, Los Angeles, into an urban farm that produces 3 tonnes of produce (vegetables, fruits and herbs) annually, with a financial turnover of around $50,000. They began by cultivating their garden to supplement their diet and sell vegetables to local restaurants. While the average American's diet requires 1.25 acres of farmland, the Dervaes feed a family of four and sell half of their crop on a pocket-size piece of land that is just 0.1 acre in size.

When Jules Dervaes and his family moved into the surburban house twenty-five years ago, he brought with him some experience in the form of a stint small-holding and beekeeping in New Zealand. But, it is only in the last decade that they have evolved their revolutionary way of life. They have successively cultivated every available square inch of earth around the house over that time, including a few hundred different types of vegetable, herbs and fruit – not to mention some livestock in the form of pygmy goats, hens and ducks. They produce enough food to meet nearly all of their needs in summer and half of them in winter. The garden is south-west facing and includes fifty raised beds, not to mention trellises for peas, beans and grapes.

The micro-scale of the farm is turned into an advantage, as the close planting discourages weeds and reduces evaporation so that the soil stays moist under the harsh Californian sun. Dervaes senior says that he is trying to take a step forwards by taking a step backwards, with the global warming crisis acting as the warning for us to live simpler lives, more in-tune with nature. They have taken the eco-mantra to reduce, re-use and recycle to its ultimate conclusion, and they can measure their food miles in inches. Additionally, they do not purchase anything they do not need, and minimize all their resources. Produce is preserved to provide supplies for the winter and all their kitchen appliances are hand- or pedal-powered. They even have a solar oven in the garden, for baking bread, which is just a box with reflectors to focus the sun's rays.

Jules Dervaes's epiphany was the accidental introduction of genetically modified corn, originally intended as animal feed, into the human food-chain about a decade ago – this inspired him to start growing as much of his own food as possible. They now supply dozens of local restaurants, and deliveries are made in a bio-diesel fuelled truck. The home-made bio-diesel cost about a dollar to make, but is very labour-intensive. The frugal but wholesome principles of the very small holding are continued in their approach to running their house, which contains no air conditioning or central heating – instead they use hot-water bottles and efficient sleeping-bags in winter. Such energy-efficiency measures mean that the recently installed photovoltaic array on their roof supplies about three-quarters of their electricity needs.

The livestock on the urban homestead are fed on vegetables, rather than petro-chemical preparations, so that odours are not a problem – they are also healthier as their immune and digestive systems are not compromised by chemicals. As well as the 3 tonnes of vegetable produce a year, over 2,000 eggs and 50lb of honey are produced annually. The Dervaes Institute ten top tips for urban farming are:

1. Grow your own food on your city plot – to provide more than half of your diet.
2. Use renewable energy sources – energy efficiency and the solar and wind.
3. Use alternative fuels and transportation – bio-fuels, bicycles and walking.
4. Keep farm animals for manure and food – practise animal husbandry.

Recycling station at the Centre for Alternative Technology (CAT) in Wales.

5. Practice waste reduction – reduce, re-use and recycle.
6. Reclaim greywater and collect rainwater – water conservation and recovery.
7. Live simply – back to basics and learn from past practices.
8. Do the work yourself – so that you learn maintenance and repair skills.
9. Work at home – develop a home-based economy.
10. Be a good neighbour – community spirit: would I want to live next to me?

The Dervaes's ambitions to change the world do not stop in their backyard, however, as the dream is to find a large piece of land and create a community of people with similar ambitions. This ambition extends to a few hundred acres and a village of sixty families, possibly in South America. The idea is that the bankrolling of the scheme, of several million dollars, is derived from future inhabitants buying their own homestead in the planned eco-utopia. Water is the key resource for such a venture, as it is a scare and expensive commodity in Southern California, where droughts can last for several months. In the Dervaes's case, this costly resource is lavished on their plants and animals, rather than themselves.

The seemingly eccentric approach of the urban homestead – 'the little house in the city' – has attracted a global following from customized websites and other means of dissemination. The publicity, including a short self-produced film called *Homegrown Revolution*, led to interest from film director Robert McFalls, who was looking for environmental heroes. The initially planned short segment became an hour-long documentary film called *Homegrown: the 21st Century Family Farm*. Hopefully, this should inspire others to start their own eco-revolution, in some small way – it all adds up.

Eco-Heroine

Joan Pick has lived an exemplary energy-efficient life for almost the last four decades, after an epiphany while working as a scientific advisor to the energy sector in the mid-1970s, and deciding to experiment with an extreme energy-efficient lifestyle – to show that it was survivable. Now in her sixties, Miss Pick has only used motorized transport twice since 1973, when she locked up her car in the garage beneath her flat in Croydon, South London. Instead she runs everywhere – 12 miles a day now, but her range was further when she was younger. Joan Pick must have one of the smallest carbon footprints on the planet, as she has lived on virtually nothing for decades. She believes she has a unique function in life – as an extreme pioneer of personal energy efficiency.

Joan Pick had her gas supply cut off a few decades ago and her electricity use is minimal, only costing several pounds a month. She eats no hot food, so has no need for a cooker or fridge – existing solely on raw food such as fruit, nuts and vegetables. Her electric kettle provides hot water for copious cups of tea and for her hand-washing, as she has no washing machine or television for that matter. As she makes her own clothes, fashion consumerism is not a problem for her.

Eco-heroine – Joan Pick.

Joan Pick knows her way around the energy question, as a maths and physics graduate from Bristol University, and she thinks we have got it wrong at the moment. She sees the earth as a business in need of sound management, with energy as the common currency and we have to live within the planet's means – there is no alternative to a fundamental change to the way we live.

Vampires and Werewolves

Electrical vampires and werewolves feed off your electricity supply as you sleep and leave electrical equipment on stand-by and over-charge mobile phones and other devices and gadgets. Several million pounds of electricity is wasted in the UK annually by leaving electrical equipment on stand-by – TVs and DVDs and the like are costing everyone pennies a day, but it all adds up. The International Energy Agency estimates that stand-by power represents nearly 10 per cent of energy demand. Manufacturers save money producing inefficient stand-by equipment, passing the running cost on to the consumer. Some appliances are worse than others, so it is worth taking a stock check with an energy monitoring device, to sort out the vampires and werewolves from the angels.

This should show LED bulbs as angels, at just 2W compared to halogen bulbs at 45W, for example. But the real vampires and werewolves are revealed when appliances are switched off. The overall effect of killing the vampires and werewolves is easily and quickly shown by installing a simple and cheap smart-metering device, which wireless-feeds data to a display showing you electricity consumption in kilowatts and kilowatt hours and pounds and pence. Primarily intended as edu-cational tools, measuring the magnetic flux around the supply wire, they are usually accurate to within plus or minus 10 per cent, and guaranteed to modify your behaviour – not to mention possibly save you tens if not hundreds of pounds.

ABOVE: **Halogen lamp with AC adaptor consuming 45W with the lamp on.**

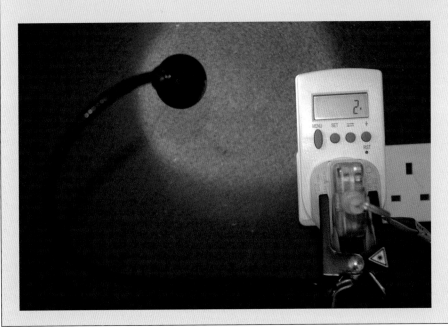

LEFT: **LED lamp consuming only 2W of electricity.**

TOP RIGHT: **Electricity monitoring device installed between the meter and consumer unit.**

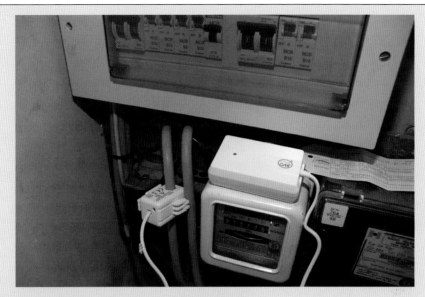

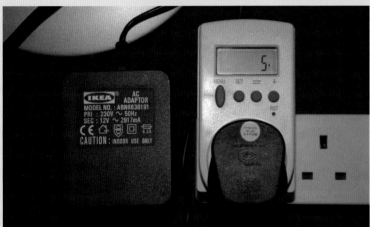

MIDDLE LEFT: **Halogen lamp with AC adaptor consuming 5W with the lamp off!**

BOTTOM LEFT: **Electricity meter – energy use in kilowatts and kilowatt hours.**

BOTTOM RIGHT: **Electricity meter – energy cost in pounds and pence.**

Appendix: Top Twenty Tips

ENERGY EFFICIENCY

1. Only use the heat, light and appliances that you really need, and buy the most energy-efficient appliances. Consider metering all supplies.
2. If you have a thermostat, try turning it down by just 1°C, as this can reduce your heating bills by 10 per cent.
3. Insulate your hot-water tank and hot-water pipes.
4. Use energy-saving lightbulbs, where appropriate (they use around a quarter of the electricity and last up to ten times longer than ordinary bulbs).
5. Make sure you have loft insulation that is at least 200mm thick.
6. Fit draughtproofing to windows and doors.
7. Improve your heating controls with timers, thermostats and thermostatic radiator valves (TRVs).
8. If you have unfilled cavity walls, and they are suitable, install cavity wall insulation.
9. If you have an old central-heating boiler, fit a modern energy-efficient boiler when the boiler needs replacement. If you have old electric storage-heaters, replace them with modern energy-efficient ones.
10. Install double-glazing when windows need replacement and, if appropriate, specify low emissivity double-glazing. Install secondary glazing, where appropriate.

ENVIRONMENTAL SUSTAINABILITY

11. Locally produced food and other supplies save on transportation pollution.
12. Turn-off lights and other electricity supplies when you are not using them. Electrical goods left on stand-by still use electricity.
13. Insulate your old house to save money and reduce carbon emissions. This and other cost-effective actions will help you to achieve a better rated energy certificate for your house.
14. Invest in white goods, such as fridges and washing-machines, with A-rated energy use.
15. Public transport is more environmentally friendly than driving a car alone.
16. Buy merchandise with minimal packaging. Packaging is energy-intensive in its production, and wasteful if it can not be recycled.
17. Reduce, re-use and recycle – glass, cans, paper and plastics. Give away old clothes and toys to support your local charity shops.
18. Write to your MP asking him or her to support measures to penalize the use of fossil fuels and give incentives to companies that use energy from renewable sources.
19. Use a water butt to collect rainwater for your garden and avoid using a hosepipe in hot weather.
20. Learn more about sustainability.

Glossary

Accreditation Scheme All Domestic Energy Assessors must be registered with an approved accreditation scheme in order to be able to register Energy Performance Certificates.

Acid rain Rain contaminated with sulphur and nitrogen in the atmosphere, largely caused by the burning of fossil fuels. The weak acidity of acid rain can corrode building materials such as limestone.

Building Research Establishment The Building Research Establishment is a former UK Government research institution and testing laboratory. It was established as the Building Research Station in 1921, with the mission of improving building and buildings. BRE was privatized in 1997 and now offers commercial, research-based consultancy to the international property and construction industries.

Biomass Biomass is anything derived from plant or animal matter and includes agricultural, forestry wastes/residues and energy crops. It can be used for fuel directly by burning or extraction of combustible oils. Biomass heating involves the use of commercial energy crops in the form of fast-growing trees, such as willow or poplar, for woodchips or waste wood products, such as sawdust, pallets or untreated recycled wood for pellets. Stand-alone stoves provide space heating for a room, and can be fitted with a back-burner to provide water heating. Boilers connected to a central heating and hot-water system are larger and usually fuelled by logs, chips and pellets.

Breather membrane A membrane that allows air and water vapour to pass through it, but which is impervious to water.

Carbon Trust The Carbon Trust is an independent not-for-profit company set up by the government with support from business to encourage and promote the development of low carbon technologies. Key to this aim is its support for UK businesses in reducing carbon emissions through funding, supporting technological innovation and by encouraging more efficient working practices. For further information visit: www. carbontrust.co.uk

Cavity wall Modern form of construction, generally appearing after about 1920, where two skins of masonry are built with a gap between them, originally connected with bricks or stones, then later by metal, stainless steel or plastic wall ties. The cavity was partially filled with insulation in new construction from about the 1980s.

CHP – Combined Heat and Power CHP is a fuel-efficient energy technology that puts to use the by-product heat that is normally wasted. Micro-CHP is a small-scale and relevant technology for domestic use. It is likely to operate in place of a domestic central-heating boiler, typically below 5kW electrical output.

Code for Sustainable Homes   The Code for Sustainable Homes is a prescriptive sustainability rating system for houses with six levels of achievement – the highest level, Level 6, equates to zero carbon. A Code rating for new houses became mandatory from 1 May 2008. The Code covers seven key areas: energy efficiency/CO_2; water efficiency; surface-water management; site-waste management; household-waste management; use of materials; and lifetime homes.

Condensing boiler   A boiler that contains a condenser to extract heat from the flue gases, and which causes water vapour in the flue gases to condense. Fuel and boiler efficiency is increased.

Conservation area   An area of special architectural or historic interest whose character and appearance it is desirable to preserve or enhance. Many nationally well-known areas are designated as conservation areas, and many of these comprise of mainly housing, such as Bedford Park in London and Saltaire in Yorkshire. Conservation areas vary greatly in their nature and character. They range from the centres of our historic towns and cities, through to Georgian and Victorian suburbs and beyond. Conservation areas give wider protection than individual listed buildings, as the special character of these areas does not come from the quality of their buildings alone. The first conservation areas were created in 1967, and there are now over 8,000 conservation areas in England. Houses in a conservation area are part of the character and history that is being preserved. As planning controls will apply, seek advice from the local planning authority early in the process. Working with the local conservation officer and a specialist design consultant will ensure the correct path of action is followed.

Conservation heating   This is an environmental strategy employed by the National Trust to conserve the historic properties and contents in their custodianship. They rarely raise the indoor temperature more than about 5°C above the temperature outdoors. This usually maintains a relative humidity (RH) in the range of 50–65 per cent, which is a good compromise for the conservation of most materials.

Dew-point temperature   The temperature at which water vapour in the air condenses to form condensation.

DPC – damp-proof course   Impervious layer of polythene, bitumen or slate laid about 150mm above ground in the base of a masonry wall to prevent rising damp.

DPM – damp-proof membrane   Impervious layer of polythene or bitumen usually laid under a concrete ground floor slab to prevent rising damp.

Embodied energy   Energy that is intrinsic to a material due to the effort that went into its extraction, processing, manufacture and transportation.

Energy Efficiency Advice Centres   A network of centres across the UK providing free, impartial and locally relevant energy-efficiency advice to householders and small businesses. Call free on 0800 512012.

EPC – Energy Performance Certificate The mandatory energy efficiency assessment component of the HIP, compiled by DEAs and Home Inspectors.

EST – Energy Saving Trust The EST is an independent not-for-profit organization, set up and largely funded by the government and the major energy companies. Its purpose is to work through partnerships towards the sustainable and efficient use of energy in the domestic and small business sectors. To this end it manages a number of programmes to improve energy efficiency, particularly in the domestic sector. For further information visit: www.energysavingtrust.org.uk

Fuel cells A fuel cell uses hydrogen and oxygen (from air) in an electrochemical reaction. Unlike technologies that 'burn' fuel, with fuel cells the conversion takes place electrochemically without combustion. Fuel cells are used in portable applications (mobile phone and laptop battery replacements), mobile applications (cars, buses, planes, etc.) and stationary applications.

Heat pumps A heat pump moves heat energy from one place to another and changes the temperature from lower to higher. An example of a commonly known heat pump is a domestic refrigerator. Where heat pumps are used for heating applications, heat is removed from the source (ambient air, water, soil or bedrock) and then discharged where the heat is needed. Where cooling is required, the reverse happens and heat is removed and discharged into air, water, soil or rock.

HECA – Home Energy Conservation Act HECA requires every UK local authority with housing responsibilities to prepare, publish and submit to the Secretary of State an energy-conservation report identifying practicable and cost-effective measures to significantly improve the energy efficiency of all residential accommodation in their area, and to report on progress made in implementing the measures.

Hydro-electric power (micro) Harnessing hydro-power at micro-power level means levels typically less than 100kW and involves utilizing naturally flowing water on land, usually rivers and streams. The type of turbine that is submerged into the water depends upon the site, geological formation of the land and flow of water present. The performance and size of micro-hydro schemes is very site specific with plant ranging from a few hundred watts to 100kW, with the higher range used for commercial schemes.

Infiltration Air entering a building accidentally and uncontrolled due to gaps and leaks in the building's fabric.

IPCC Intergovermental Panel on Climate Change

kW – kilowatt Unit of power (kW) equivalent to 1,000W or 1.34 horsepower.

kWh – kilowatt hour Unit of energy consumption (kWh) equivalent to using 1kW of energy for an hour.

Kyoto Protocol A protocol to the UN Framework Convention on Climate Change (UNFCCC) agreed in 1997. Developed nations are required to cut overall greenhouse gas emissions by an average of 5.2 per cent below 1990 levels over the period 2008–2012.

LED – light emitting diode Solid-state light source that emits light or invisible infrared radiation when electricity is passed through it.

Listed building The term 'listing' is used to describe a number of procedures used to protect our architectural heritage. When houses are listed they are placed on a statutory list of houses of 'special architectural or historic interest'. The older and rarer a house is, the more likely it is to be listed. Houses less than thirty years older are rarely listed, but increasing numbers of post-war buildings are now being listed. In England and Wales, listed buildings are classified as:

- Grade I – buildings of exceptional interest and national significance.
- Grade II* – buildings of particular importance of more than special interest.
- Grade II – buildings of special interest, warranting every effort to preserve them.

Scotland and Northern Ireland use similar classifications, labelled A, B and C. The local planning department (which may have a conservation officer) will determine the specific requirements for any work proposed to historic homes. The type of work requiring Listed Building Consent varies with the building classification.

LNG – liquefied natural gas   When natural gas is cooled to a temperature of approximately −160°C at atmospheric pressure it condenses to a liquid called liquefied natural gas (LNG). Natural gas is composed primarily of methane (typically, at least 90 per cent), but may also contain ethane, propane and heavier hydrocarbons.

Low-emissivity (low-E) glazing   Glazing with a very thin metallic film on the side facing the building interior, which reflects some of the heat back into the room – improving the U-value of the glazing and leading to higher energy efficiency.

LPG – liquefied petroleum gas   Gas, usually propane or butane, derived from oil and put under pressure so that it is in liquid form. Often used to power portable cooking stoves or heaters and to fuel some types of vehicle, e.g. some specially adapted road vehicles and forklift trucks.

NHER – National Home Energy Rating Scheme   The UK's first and largest quality assured energy rating scheme – owned by National Energy Services.

Night setback   A feature of a room thermostat that allows a lower temperature to be maintained outside the period during which the normal room temperature is required.

NT – National Trust   The NT is a UK charity that relies for income on membership fees, donations and legacies, and revenue raised from commercial operations. They protect and open to the public over 300 historic houses and gardens, and nearly fifty industrial monuments and mills. The NT also looks after forests, woods, fens, beaches, farmland, downs, moorland, islands, archaeological remains, castles, nature reserves and villages.

Passivhaus Standard   Passivhaus is a set of stringent guidelines to achieve low-carbon houses, which use 90 per cent less than average dwellings, based on robust building physics. The approach includes data analysis using a software package called PHPP (PassivHaus Plannning Package). Passivhaus design seeks to minimize space heating and cooling as the most robust way of reducing carbon emissions. Heat losses are reduced by super-insulating, reducing thermal bridges and air leakage, and mechanically ventilating with heat recovery. Total energy demand for space heating must be less than $15kWh/m^2/year$.

Payback period   The period of time that has to elapse before the capital cost of an energy efficiency investment is repaid by savings. Simple payback is usually used, which does not take the future value of money into account.

Pressure test   Air pressure is tested in a building to determine the airtightness of the building fabric. A fan blows air into a doorway and measures the volume of air delivered to maintain a given pressure.

Prevailing wind   The direction from which the wind usually blows – generally from the southwest in the British Isles. Cold and fast winds can also often come from the north or north-east.

PV – photovoltaics   The direct conversion of solar radiation into electricity by the interaction of light with the electrons in a semiconductor device or cell.

PVC   Poly vinyl chloride.

PVC-u   Unplasticized PVC or rigid PVC.

RH – relative humidity   This is a measure of the quantity of moisture in the air, shown as a percentage of the maximum amount it could hold at the same temperature. Cold air can hold less moisture than warm air, so the RH in a room will increase as the temperature falls. An RH of 50–65 per cent is a good compromise for the conservation of most materials.

Renewable energy   Renewable energy includes solar power, wind, wave and tide, and hydro-electricity. Solid renewable energy sources consist of energy crops, other biomass, wood, straw and waste, whereas gaseous renewables consist of landfill gas and sewage waste.

Renewables Obligation   The obligation placed on licensed electricity suppliers to deliver a specified amount of their electricity from eligible renewable sources.

Room thermostat   A sensing device to measure the air temperature within a room and regulate the space heating. A single target temperature may be set by the user.

SAP Rating – Standard Assessment Procedure Rating   The energy performance of individual houses is measured using the Government's Standard Assessment Procedure (SAP), a rating scale of 1 to 100, in which 100 represents the best performance possible. SAP takes account of the fuel efficiency of heating systems and the thermal efficiency of the building fabric (i.e. how well it retains heat in winter). It also takes account of other factors including the type of construction (e.g. cavity wall, solid wall, terraced, semi-detached, detached or flat), the shape, size and orientation of the house, and the size and distribution of windows. A version of SAP, known as reduced data Standard Assessment Procedure (rdSAP), is used to measure performance for Energy Performance Certificate ratings.

SEDBUK – Seasonal Efficiency of Domestic Boilers in the UK   An online database that contains performance data on over 3,000 boilers (www.sedbuk.com).

Solar photovoltaic (PV) electricity generation   Photovoltaic generates electricity from sunlight. Small-scale modules are available as roof-mounted panels, roof tiles and conservatory or atrium roof systems. The performance of a PV system will depend on the size of the system, the type of PV cell used and the nature of the installation. A typical domestic system may produce enough electricity to supply almost half of an average family's annual supply.

Solar thermal hot water heating   Solar thermal is the most commonly installed form of solar energy currently in use. It can typically provide almost all hot water requirements during summer months and about 50 per cent all year round. There are three main components for domestic hot-water systems: solar panels, a heat transfer system and a hot-water cylinder. The solar panels, or collectors, are usually fitted to the roof and collect heat from the sun's radiation. This heat is used to raise the temperature of the household water and is delivered by the heat transfer system, which takes the heated water to the hot-water cylinder for storage until use.

Sustainability   Sustainable development is progress that 'meets the needs of the present without compromising the ability of future generations to meet their own needs'. This is the Brundtland definition of sustainability.

Temperature and time zone control   A control scheme that makes it possible to select different temperatures at different times in two (or more) different zones.

Thermal break   An element of low conductivity placed within material of higher conductivity in order to reduce rate of heat flow though the building element, such as a window frame.

Thermal bridge A continuous element of building fabric that spans from the inside of the house to the outside and acts as a route for heat flow and loss, such as a continuous window sill or lintel.

Thermal mass Dense material, such as stone, concrete or brickwork, which can store heat. This accounts for the cool interiors, on hot sunny days, of thermally heavyweight buildings with thick stone walls, such as cathedrals. Thermal mass in houses can help to prevent excessive heat from solar gains in summer, but will generally take longer to heat up in winter than thermally lightweight houses.

Thermostat An electronic device that measures temperature, and in the case of a house, maintains room temperature at a set point controlled by occupants.

Thermostatic radiator valve A radiator valve with an air temperature sensor, used to control the heat output from the radiator by adjusting water flow.

Time switch An electrical switch operated by a clock to control either space heating or hot water, or both together but not independently. The user chooses one or more 'on' periods, usually in a daily or weekly cycle.

Trickle vent A small adjustable opening, usually placed in window frames, that allows building occupants to control background ventilation.

U-value A U-value is an indication of how much heat is conducted through a particular section of building construction. The lower the U-value, the better insulated the structure is. For example, a wall with a U-value of $1.0W/m^2K$ will lose heat twice as fast as a wall with a U-value of $0.5W/m^2K$. The rate of heat loss is measured in watts (W) per square metre (m^2) for every degree of temperature difference (K) between the inner and outer surfaces of the wall.

Vernacular architecture Pragmatic construction, usually house-building, in regional styles with local materials and craftsmanship – usually involving prosaic reactions to local weather, materials and customs.

Weather compensator A device, or feature within a device, that adjusts the temperature of the water circulating through the heating system according to the temperature measured outside the building.

Wind turbines (micro) Wind turbines harness the wind to produce electrical power. The efficiency of a domestic system will depend on factors such as location and surrounding environment and the electricity output is usually between 2.5 and 6kWs, but can be as low as 1kW. The latest development in domestic wind turbine technology is roof-mounted turbines for installation on domestic dwellings. These mini-wind turbines give a nominal output of 1kW and are designed to generate energy from low wind speeds. They are typically mounted on the gable end of buildings although in some cases can be attached to the building side-walls.

Zone control A control scheme in which it is possible to select different times and/or temperatures in two (or more) different zones.

Further Information

BOOKS

Anderson, W. (2007). *Green up! An A–Z of environmentally friendly home improvements.*

Berners-Lee, M. (2010). *How bad are bananas: the carbon footprint of everything.*

Berry, S. (2007). *Fifty ways to save water and energy.*

Borer, P. & Harris, C. (2005) *The whole house book: ecological building design and materials.*

Brand, S. (1994). *How buildings learn: what happens after they're built.*

Brand, S. (2009). *Whole earth discipline: an ecopragmatist manifesto.*

Brassington, M. (2007). *How to go carbon neutral.*

Brereton, C. (1995). *The repair of historic buildings: advice on principles and methods.*

Bridgewater, A. & G. (2008). *The off-grid energy handbook.*

Bridgewater, A. & G. (2009). *The self-sufficiency handbook.*

Broome, J. (2007). *The green self-build book: how to design and build your own eco-home.*

Brown, G.Z. (1985). *Sun, wind and light: architectural design strategies.*

Callard, S. (2008). *The little green book of the home: 250 tips for an eco lifestyle.*

Carson, R. (1962). *Silent spring.*

CAT (2010). *Zero-carbon Britain 2030.*

Cook, M.G. (2009). *Energy efficiency in old houses.*

Clegg, B. (2007). *The global warming survival kit.*

Clift, J. & Cuthbert, A. (2006). *Energy, use less – save more: 100 energy saving tips for the home.*

Davies, A. (2007). *Beekeeping.*

Dawson, J. (2006). *Ecovillages: new frontiers for sustainability.*

DCLG. (2006). *Code for sustainable homes: a step change in sustainable home building practice.*

DCLG. (2008). *Code for sustainable homes: technical guide.*

De Rothschild, D. (2007). *The live earth global warming handbook.*

Desai, P. (2010). *One planet communities: a real-life guide to sustainable living.*

Dow, K. & Downing, T.E. (2006). *The atlas of climate change: mapping the world's greatest challenge.*

Dunster, W. et al. (2007). *The ZEDbook: solutions for a shrinking world.*

Eastoe, J. (2007). *Henkeeping.*

Eastoe, J. (2009). *Allotments.*

European Commission (1996). *The climatic dwelling: an introduction to climate-responsive residential architecture.*

Falk, A. et al. (2007). *Photovoltaics for professionals: solar electric systems marketing, design and installation.*

Farris, J. (2005). *Ten minute energy saving secrets.*

Foley, G. (1976). *The energy question.*

Galligan, D. (2007). *Home-grown vegetables.*

Goodall, C. (2007). *How to live a low carbon life.*

Goodstein, D. (2004). *Out of gas: the end of the age of oil.*

Gore, A. (2006). *An inconvenien t truth: the planetary emergency of global warming and what we can do about it.*

Goulding, J.R. et al. (eds). (1992). *Energy conscious design: a primer for architects.*

Grant, N. et al. (2005). *Sewage solutions: answering the call of nature.*

Griffiths, N. (2007). *Eco-house manual.*

Harland, E. (2004). *Eco-renovation: the ecological home improvement guide.*

Harper, G. (2009). *Domestic solar energy: a guide for the homeowner.*

Harper, P. & Halestrap, L. (1999). *Lifting the lid: an ecological approach to toilet systems.*

Henson, R. (2006). *The rough guide to climate change.*

Hewitt, M. & Telfer, K. (2007). *Earthships: building a zero carbon future for homes.*

Hillman, M. (2004). *How can we save the planet?*

Hobson, J. & Rant, P. (2009). *Successful smallholding: planning, starting and managing your enterprise.*

Hopkins, R. (2008). *The transition handbook: from oil dependence to local resilience.*

Hyde, R. (ed.). (2008). *Bioclimatic housing: innovative designs for warm climates.*

Hymers, P. (2006). *Converting to an eco-friendly home.*

Kerridge, D. (2008). *Off the grid: managing independent renewable energy systems.*

Jackson, A. & Day, D. (2005). *Period house: how to repair, restore and care for your home.*

Johnson, A. (1984). *How to restore and improve your Victorian house.*

Langley, W. & Curtis, D. (2004). *Going with the flow: small scale water power.*

Laughton, C. (2006). *Tapping the sun: a guide to solar water heating.*

Laughton, C. (2006). *Home heating with wood.*

Laws, A. (2003). *Understanding small period houses.*

Liddel, H. (2008). *Eco-minimalism: the antidote to eco-bling.*

Littler, J. & Thomas, R. (1984). *Design with energy: the conservation and use of energy in buildings.*

Lloyd, S. (2008). *The carbon diaries 2015.*

Lovelock, J. (1979). *Gaia: a new look at life on earth.*

Lovelock, J. (1988). *The ages of Gaia: a biography of our living earth.*

Lovelock, J. (2000). *Homage to Gaia: the life of an independent scientist.*

Lovelock, J. (2006). *The revenge of Gaia.*

Lovelock, J. (2009). *The vanishing face of Gaia: a final warning.*

Lynas, M. (2007). *Carbon counter: calculate your carbon footprint.*

Lynas, M. (2008). *Six degrees: our future on a hotter planet.*

Mackay, D.J.C. (2008). *Sustainable energy – without the hot air.*

Mazria, E. (1979). *The passive solar energy handbook.*

McCrea, A. (2008). *Renewable energy: a user's guide.*

Meyer, A. (2000). *Contraction and convergence: the global solution to climate change.*

Monbiot, G. (2007). *Heat: how we can stop the planet burning.*

Neder, F. (2008). *Fuller houses: R Buckminster Fuller's dymaxion dwellings and other domestic adventures.*

Oxley, R. (2003). *Survey and repair of traditional buildings: a sustainable approach.*

Pearson, D. (1989). *The natural house book: creating a healthy, harmonious and ecologically sound home.*

Piggot, H. (2006). *Choosing windpower.*

Ramage, J. (1983). *Energy: a guide book.*

Reynolds, M. (1989). *A coming of wizards.*

Reynolds, M. (1990). *Earthship volume 1: how to build your own.*

Reynolds, M. (1991). *Earthship volume 2: systems and components.*

Reynolds, M. (1993). *Earthship volume 3: evolution beyond economics.*

Reynolds, M. (2000). *Comfort in any climate.*

Reynolds, M. (2005). *Water from the sky.*

Roaf, S. et al. (2004). *Closing the loop: benchmarks for sustainable buildings.*

Roaf, S. et al. (2007). *Ecohouse: a design guide.*

Rock, I.A. (2007). *The 1930s house manual.*

Rock, I.A. (2007). *The Victorian house manual.*

Rosen, N. (2008). *How to live off-grid.*

Royal Commission on Environmental Pollution. (1997). *Energy: the changing climate.*

Ryker, L. (2007). *Off the grid homes: case studies for sustainable living.*

Salomon, T. & Bedel, S. (2007). *The energy saving house.*

Scott, N. (2005). *Reduce, re-use, recycle: an easy household guide.*

Seymour, J. (1975). *The complete book of self-sufficiency.*

SPAB/IHBC. (2002). *A stitch in time: maintaining your property makes good sense and saves money.*

Strahan, D. (2007). *The last oil shock: a survival guide to the imminent extinction of petroleum man.*

Thornton, J. (2007). *The water book: find it, move it, store it, clean it ... use it.*

Trimby, P. (2000). *Solar water heating.*

Vale, R. & B. (1975). *The autonomous house: designing and planning for self-sufficiency.*

Vale, R. & B. (2000). *The new autonomous house: designing and planning for sustainability.*

Van der Ryn, S. (1978). *The toiler papers: recycling waste and conserving water.*

Waterfield, P. (2006). *The energy efficient home: a complete guide.*

White, N. (2008). *Saving energy in the home.*

Winblad, U. & Kilama, W. (1978). *Sanitation without water.*

Woolley, T. (2006). *Natural building: a guide to materials and techniques.*

Yannis, S. (1994). *Solar energy and house design: principles, objectives, guidelines* (vol. 1).

Yannis, S. (1994). *Solar energy and house design: examples* (vol. 2).

ENERGY SAVING TRUST PUBLICATIONS

GIR 38. (1995). *Review of ultra-low-energy homes: a series of UK and overseas profiles.*

GIR 53. (1995). *Building a sustainable future: homes for an autonomous community.*

GIR 39. (1996). *Review of ultra-low-energy homes: ten UK profiles in detail.*

GIR 89. (2001). *BedZED – Beddington zero energy development, Sutton.*

GIR 72. (2002). *Energy efficiency standards – for new and existing dwellings.*

USEFUL WEBSITES

Association for Environment-Conscious Buildings – www.aecb.net

Buckminster Fuller – www.bfi.org

Building Research Establishment – www.bre.org.uk

Cadw – www.cadw.wales.gov.uk

Climate Change – www.climatechange.eu.com

Code for Sustainable Homes – www.communities.gov.uk

Energy Saving Trust – www.est.org.uk

English Heritage – www.english-heritage.org.uk

Environment Agency – www.environment-agency.gov.uk

Environment & Heritage Service, Northern Ireland – www.ehsni.gov.uk

Georgian Group – www.georgiangroup.org.uk

Global warming – www.globalwarming.com

Greenpeace – www.greenpeace.org.uk

Heath and Safety Executive – www.hse.gov.uk

Historic Scotland – www.historic-scotland.gov.uk

Landmark Trust – www.landmarktrust.org.uk

National Inventory of Architectural Heritage, Ireland – www.buildingsofireland.ie

National Trust – www.nationaltrust.org.uk

National Trust for Scotland – www.nts.org.uk

Passivhaus – www.passivehouse.com

RIBA Register of Architects Accredited in Building Conservation – www.aabc-register.co.uk

Royal Incorporation of Architects in Scotland – www.rias.org.uk

Royal Institute of British Architects – www.riba.org

Royal Institute of Chartered Surveyors – www.rics.org.uk

SAVE Britain's Heritage – www.savebritainsheritage.org

SEDBUK – www.boilers.org.uk

Smart metering – www.readyourmeter.org

Society for the Protection of Ancient Buildings – www.spab.org.uk

Sustainable Energy – www.withouthotair.com

Sustainable Energy Ireland (SEI) – www.sei.ie

Twentieth Century Society – www.c20society.org.uk

Vernacular Architecture Group – www.vag.org.uk

Victorian Society – www.victorian-society.org.uk

FILMS

Documentary

A convenient truth: urban solutions from Curitiba, Brazil (2007). Directed by Maria Terezinha Vaz.

An inconvenient truth (2006). Directed by Davis Guggenheim.

Building with awareness: the construction of a hybrid home (2005). Directed by Ted Owens.

Garbage Warrior (2008). Directed by Oliver Hodge.

Fast food nation. (2007). Directed by Richard Linklater.

Home (2010). Directed by Yann Arthus-Bertrand.

Last call for planet earth: architects for a better world (2008). Directed by Jacques Allard. European Commission for Energy.

McLibel (2005). Directed by Franny Armstong and Ken Loach.

Our daily bread (2005). Directed by Nikolaus Geyrhalter.

Six degrees could change the world (2008). Directed by Ron Bowman. National Geographic.

The age of stupid (2009). Directed by Fanny Armstrong.

The cove (2009). Directed by Louie Psihoyos.

The eleventh hour: turn mankind's darkest hour into its finest (2008). Directed by Leila Conners Peterson.

The end of the line (2009). Directed by Rupert Murray.

The great global warming swindle (2007). Directed by Martin Durkin.

The truth about climate change (2006). Directed by David Attenborough.

Vanishing of the bees (2009). Directed by George Langworthy and Maryam Henein.

Who killed the electric car? (2006). Directed by Chris Paine.

Fiction

Logan's run (1976). Directed by Michael Anderson.

Silent running (1972). Directed by Douglas Trumbull.

Soylent green (1973). Directed by Richard Fleischer.

Index

RELATED TITLES FROM CROWOOD

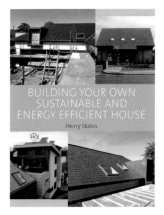

Building Your Own Sustainable and Energy Efficient House

HENRY SKATES

ISBN 978 1 84797 258 3

192pp, 155 illustrations

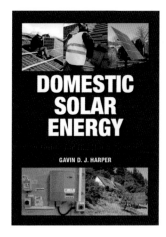

Domestic Solar Energy

GAVIN D.J. HARPER

ISBN 978 1 84797 060 2

128pp, 160 illustrations

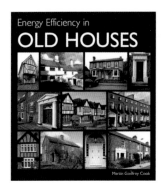

Energy Efficiency in Old Houses

MARTIN GODFREY COOK

ISBN 978 1 84797 077 0

160pp, 100 illustrations

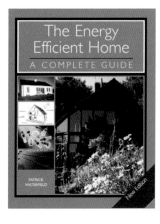

Energy Efficient Home

PATRICK WATERFIELD

ISBN 978 1 84797 259 0

176pp, 80 illustrations

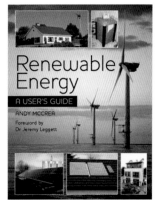

Renewable Energy

ANDY McCREA

ISBN 978 1 86126 061 9

160pp, 100 illustrations

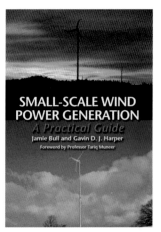

Small-Scale Wind Power Generation

JAMIE BULL and GAVIN D.J. HARPER

ISBN 978 1 84797 210 1

144pp, 140 illustrations